Contents

Foreword. . . . .

Groundwork-early railways. . . . . P. 5

The first line to Harrogate. . . . . P. 12

Hints of a new line. . . . . P. 15

The East & West Yorks. Junction Railway. . . . . . . P. 24

The line described - Poppleton Jc. to Hammerton. . P. 25

The line described - Cattal to Goldsborough. . . . . . P. 32

Knaresborough - environs and history. . . . . P. 41

Starbeck and Harrogate. P. 44

Passenger services. . . . . P. 50

Motive power. . . . . P. 59

Timetables, plans and railwayana. . . . . P. 63

Abbreviations used:

Y & NMR	York and North Midland Railway.
L & ThR	Leeds & Thirsk Railway.
NER	North Eastern Railway.
SO SX	Saturdays only/excepted.
MWFO	Mondays, Wednesdays, Fridays Only.

Foreword

I should mention the difficulties which are often met with in trying to raise track layouts for use in these books. They are, more often than not, taken from large scale O/S maps in the larger libraries - here York and Northallerton, but invariably they are of different ages, with perhaps one missing, or only half a railway station where such lies on the edge of two sheets. In the case here nearly all are for the 1910 period, though one must remember that alterations were often made to layouts in subsequent years. Signalling diagrams have been included in three cases.

The photographs in this work have suffered through the sad death recently, of Mr. L. Smith of Len's of Sutton; I am certain that several interesting shots of the line would have been willingly sent from that direction. Instead I have enjoyed several trips, often with walks attached, into the balmy air of the region to obtain my own specimens - though no steam efforts! I have used as historical reference W.W. Tomlinson's 'North Eastern Railway' and a fascinating and newsy little book by Mr James Rodgers on the railways of Harrogate, full of much material which remains to be used by others.

My grateful thanks as usual to the Local Studies departments of the York, Northallerton, Harrogate, Hull and Devon libraries, the latter for the timetables used. Thanks also to the Ken Hoole Collection curator at North Road, Darlington.

Alas, no gradient profile of the line has surfaced as yet.

C.T. GOODE.
Anlaby, 2001.

1. Groundwork - Early Railways in the area.

To begin the railway history surrounding a particular area is always a difficult task to pursue, especially in this case and particularly with Harrogate and Knaresborough, where two or three powerful promoters were in contention. Throughout the country this financial and at times political warfare was taking place as part of the so-called 'Railway Mania', where party A would propose a perfectly good scheme to link two places, only to have it challenged by party B who, possessed by more money than sense, would offer its own scheme which would be more grandiose, than the first. The prime object would be to block the intentions of the first party, to confuse the interests of the town involved or, quite simply to make a grand gesture and display altruism and a certain arrogance. Thus, the Mania produced at least one idea for a channel tunnel and a Humber bridge, neither backed up by substantial surveys or common sense. So it was in the Harrogate and Knaresborough area, with the latter town, altogether more comely and lively playing a greater part much earlier (1802) than did the more dowdy Harrogate which was left on the shelf for much longer, blocked out by immense engineering problems to the south. I shall, therefore, only refer to rival schemes if they did seem to stand a chance of being successful.

It is necessary, first of all, to touch on the first railways to appear in the Yorkshire area before the York-Harrogate line came into being. The initial line was the Leeds & Selby Railway of 1834, running to a terminus on the town side of the Ouse in Selby. This was followed by the Hull & Selby, opened in 1840, which produced a lifting bridge over the river and a logical linking of the two lines together to form a good and level route between Hull's docks and Leeds's commerce. Terms will need to be watched from now on, as this route became part of the greater York & North Midland Railway, a concern in which George Hudson of York was to become much involved, and which ran up from Derby, through Normanton to Leeds and York from 1839. The two

D49 No. 62752 'The Atherstone' runs into Hopperton on a through York - Harrogate train. Here the line crosses the A1 - the gates would have been worked from the box as they were double on each side. On the left side near the wicket is a single lever rod and an old turning wheel. For what purpose is not obvious.

Photograph Copyright by: J.W. Armstrong Trust.

routes crossed neatly at Milford Jc., near the site of today's Selby coal sidings.

York was now on the railway map and this was more firmly fixed on the map by the run of the Great North of England Railway, down from Newcastle and over its origins on the Stockton & Darlington Railway, all fostered by Joseph Pease, in a straight line to the walled city from March 1841. The original idea was to run to a point three miles west of York, with a branch serving the city proper, though this ramification was short lived. George Stephenson was the engineer responsible for much of the work which included a junction near Thirsk with a long branch through Boroughbridge, Knaresborough and Tadcaster, to Leeds, where the York & North Midland would be joined. 'Near Thirsk' could have originally meant Thirsk station, which was quite a way out of the town where a branch did in fact lead off via Melmerby, or Pilmoor Jc. to the south which went direct to Boroughbridge and Knaresborough. In the event both were built, the latter never amounting to much. The York & North Mid. which now had branched into the city from Scarborough and Hull, felt that they could exert some leverage over what might be afoot and asked for the GN of E line to enter York via Skelton over an Ouse bridge which might be shared with their own trains So it came about, and Joseph Pease, a man of vision, could murmur of trains reaching 60 mph. over a four track section between Darlington and York.

The Harrogate bay at York. *C.T. Goode.*

Next followed a little of the sabre-rattling mentioned at the beginning: as also mentioned, the GN of ER had planned for a branch from Pilmoor to Boroughbridge, Knaresborough and Harrogate, probably soft pedalling the other route from Thirsk. All the same a vociferous band of Leeds folk proposed in 1844 a route running the other way to Thirsk, with branches to Harrogate and Knaresborough, thus bringing Starbeck potentially into heavy use. The GN of E countered with an extension of the Pilmoor- Harrogate branch to Leeds via Spofforth, anticipating the Wetherby-Crossgates line by many years; however George Hudson had by now taken over the GN of E to add to the Y & NM, so that the latter bill was withdrawn and the new Leeds faction found itself with a free run. The Act was approved on 21st. July 1845 and what became the Leeds and Thirsk Railway was formed, the first section opening from Ripon to Thirsk (Town) in 1848, followed by Wormald Green to Ripon and Wormald Green to Weeton, including Starbeck which opened on 19th. September 1848 to serve Harrogate and Knaresborough. The stage south of Weeton with its heavy engineering was to open much later. An Act put forward by the York & Newcastle (former GN of E) in 1846 included a branch from the Pilmoor-Boroughbridge branch which had been part of the original line to Harrogate. This was 5 3/4 miles southwards and was opened by the Y & N on 17th. June 1847. Boroughbridge was not to be linked to Knaresborough until 1875.

At this stage Harrogate was still without a railway, as was Knaresborough, though thoughts had turned in that direction, an idea perhaps not unusual for a place that was the birthplace of John Metcalfe, born in 1711, soon blind and a self-instructed bridge and road maker. Outdoor life must have suited him, for he lived to the age of 93. In 1802 a line of 1 1/2 miles was planned to run from the town to Cold Keld near Scriven to the north. This was to meet with a canal from here to Ellenthorp Shoals near Boroughbridge and ultimately reach the Tees and its coal by a further canal. The project foundered due to lack of money for a second canal.

Poppleton station. Note the catchers on the roof edges to protect the glasswork.   *C.T. Goode.*

Undaunted, in 1818 another canal survey was carried out by Thomas Telford to two points, one to the Ouse below Linton lock, the other to the Wharfe above Tadcaster. The aim this time was to ferry cheap coal not from the Tees, but from the West Riding. These failed because of the number of locks involved, so like all good fairy stories a third attempt was made, this time with a proposal for a canal to the Ouse at Acaster Selby from a point at Ribston Green on Crimple beck, linked from here to Knaresborogh at a cost of £93,000. Apparently the reason for the failure of this plan was that a railway line could be laid along the line of route for £60,000 and on to Pateley Bridge for an extra £30,000. In 1820 support was canvassed for yet another railway mooted from Bolton Percy which would convey cheap coal and flax for the local spinning mills, as well as passengers if brave enough. This idea was also consigned to limbo, finally losing a small dream of early steam power which, if brought into being, would have beaten the Stockton & Darlington by five years.

Hessay station. Note the open air lever frame and remains of a telegraph post.   *C.T. Goode.*

In 1844 the Leeds & Thirsk made a proposal for a line which would run through Starbeck and Ripon to Thirsk but avoid Knaresborough. In the same year the GN of E modified their plans for a line to Leeds because of the terrain between Horsforth and Weeton; instead they concentrated on a route from Pilmoor to Harrogate via Boroughbridge, with a branch to Ripon, to be known as the Harrogate & Ripon Jc. Railway. This would have skirted Knaresborough, ending at Collin's Cottage on Wetherby road, two miles south east of Harrogate. The GN of E then asked the Leeds and Thirsk to give up their plans northwards and, instead construct their line on to Leeds from Wetherby. They refused, leaving the GN of E to construct this line themselves. On 19th. December 1844 a meeting of Knaresborough residents met to discuss the L & T plans, which included a branch to Starbeck, including a gradient of

The site of Wilstrop Siding. C.T. Goode.

1 in 103 and curves. These were unsuitable points for passenger trains! The GN of E had exaggerated the steepness of gradients on the proposed L & T main line, so no doubt this element had been used also in demeaning the branch line details. Nevertheless the L & T were undaunted and promised to link Knaresborough with both north and south and bring in the town's coal at 6/8- (33p) per ton. (The GN of E were charging 12/- (60p) per ton at Thirsk). The result was that ultimately Knaresborough supported what the L & T were offering.

Once George Hudson became Chairman of both the Y & NM and GN of E railways the Harrogate & Ripon scheme was scotched, most likely to dissuade the L & T from pressing with an Act of their own, as happened on 21st. July 1845, a clear case of negative blocking.

2. The first line to Harrogate.

Harrogate was about to obtain a railway of its own from another direction, quite surprising as a great deal of money and energy were to be spent on reaching one quite modest town. The Y & NM had surveyed a line from Church Fenton, an almost unknown village on the York-Normanton line, to Harrogate, in September 1845. This was successful apart from the Harrogate end, where two level crossings of the Hookstone and Leeds roads would bring its course too close to the Tewitt well in High Harrogate. This had to be altered so as to pass as far from the Stray as possible. The line opened from Church Fenton to Spofforth on 10th. August 1847, where some 100 navvies lived in a shanty town near to Prospect tunnel (286yd.) near Crimple. Men were set to work on Sundays and were attacked by local folk for this desecration of the Sabbath, as well as by their own church-going workmates who had foregone a sixpence per hour rise for the labours. In October 1847 most of the workforce were laid off for the winter, while the Crimple viaduct, 110 ft. high and 1,873 ft. long was completed on 23rd. December of that year.

Hammerton station. The signalman leaves the 'Victorian firescreen'.   *C.T. Goode.*

Opening the gates at Hammerton - notice the length.
C.T. Goode.

The Brunswick station, named after a nearby hotel, was approached through a long single line tunnel of 286 yd., an additional thrill after the viaduct, to reach the station site on which the line ran to a single platform and crude buildings facing the present B6162 adjacent to the Prince of Wales roundabout. A goods line branched off left, forking into two to arrive at the road way. On the north side of Trinity Road is a memorial stone, worth a look if one is prepared to negotiate the roundabout which is very busy. The tunnel is still present beneath Longcliffe Avenue, with the portal beyond St. George's Road roundabout now filled in. At the other end the portal is too far from the present railway to be easily spotted through the undergrowth. The station buildings were of wood, derived in part from farm buildings already on the site. There were no watering facilities, either for engine or passenger, the first finding sustenance way back at Prospect tunnel. From the track layout it would appear to have been difficult to run the engine round its train unless a spare engine was left at Brunswick to help in this. More likely, the empty stock was either manhandled into position, or marshalled by horse power. The station, opened on 20th. July 1848, had five station masters in its short life, the first being Mr. Gowling, late captain in the 72nd. Highlanders. In 1855 a booking clerk was arrested for embezzlement, perhaps proving that the takings were up to scratch.

At the outset Harrogate was dependent on Starbeck for services to Leeds and the North. This was about two miles from the town, a distance covered by omnibuses which were poor and expensive, manned by often rude conductors. Brunswick did in fact lie close to the town centre, but trains could take 1hr. 50min. to York and Leeds and 4hr. 15min. to Scarborough, all with a wait to change at Church Fenton; over the years this station became disproportionally huge for the amount of traffic, with four main platforms and a fine array of trackwork. The local newspaper bemoaned Harrogate's isolation, the poor service between Starbeck and Knaresborough, reluctance of the station staff at Ripon to help passengers and paradoxically of trains being run on Sundays. Thousands saw Queen Victoria go north in 1858, through Starbeck station after opening Leeds Town Hall. Charles Dickens visited Harrogate in 1858, hiring a train to take him to York. His brother, a railway engineer, designed the Malton and Driffield railway and lived in the former town.

3. Hints of a new line.

In 1845 the pompous sounding East & West Yorkshire Junction Railway had obtained an Act in Parliament to build a railway of 15 ¼ miles from York to Knaresborough, with permission to use York station. The line was constructed without serious problems and opened in March 1848 as far as the east side of Knaresborough, just short of the site of the tunnel. Eventually the engineers overcame this routine obstacle and carried on to Starbeck, being eventually opened throughout on 1st. October 1851 after the reconstruction of the Nidd viaduct which had collapsed.
It would be pleasant to think that perhaps Dickens had his special train routed over this line, lending a touch of distinction to the type of passenger conveyed.

At long last, on 31st. July 1854 the North Eastern Railway came into being, sweeping away the often petty little concerns which now came together beneath one large umbrella with head offices in York. The work on the Leeds end of the line to Thirsk had been given to the contractor James Bray and divided into two sections, Leeds-Horsforth and Horsforth-Weeton, beginning on 20th. October 1845 with the digging of a shaft at Bramhope tunnel where, due chiefly to the release of millions of gallons of water, a way could only be forced through on 27th. November 1848. However, the tunnel, of 3,761 yd. was eventually opened for through traffic on 19th. September 1854, then closed again, due to the collapse of part of the interior. A passenger train ran into the debris with five of the carriages running back down the 1 in 94 gradient to Arthington, being stopped by the efficient handling of the brake by the guard. Unfortunately a sixth coach ran back separately and caused a pile-up, though happily, no fatalities. The line could be reopened on 1st. January 1855 to serve its purpose of shortening the distance to Leeds by 14 miles.

Probably the best one of the lot. Cattal station c. 1973.
C.T. Goode.

The NER next decided to construct the long awaited line from Starbeck south to a point just outside the south end of Brunswick tunnel, along with other lines from Bilton to Dragon Jc. and an important spur from Pannal up and round to the east end of Crimple viaduct. For Harrogate the icing on the cake would be a brand new station. Knaresborough folk objected to the developments because they felt that they would have to travel further and pay more to catch a main line service. Harrogate burghers also grumbled, this time because the new line would need to cross the Stray. To this the NER countered by promising to give up the Brunswick station site and branch in compensation for the Stray land taken, the new line to be in shallow cutting as seen today.

Work began on these welcome refinements in October 1860, though not immediately on the Pannal-Crimple section as the weather became severe, with workmen laid off and transferred to snow clearing, in order to keep some sort of wage coming in. However, by 1862 work was again in full swing. In the town a bridge was included spanning Bower Road, north of the station in readiness for future developments in High Harrogate. This collapsed before completion, delaying the line's opening until 1st. August 1862. This delay damped the ardour of many who would have assembled to herald the arrival of a new train service, though there were celebrations at places where the railway could now reach, with garlands of flowers on the Pateley Bridge branch, a run-to-be of 40 minutes from Harrogate, and at Nidd Bridge and Ripley Valley on the Leeds Northern. Starbeck was also not to be left out of things.

On the opening day Brunswick station closed, remaining in use as a goods depot for a few months until facilities were completed at the new station, known as Central. Only one platform was in use at first, with some Leeds trains returning on a circular run via Starbeck for a time. Knaresborough no doubt rejoiced when the station there was rebuilt in 1865, before which time in the same year a loop was put in between Belmont Crossing and Stonefall round to the south by the engine shed to allow trains to travel between Pannal and Knaresborough, thus avoiding the bustle of Starbeck. This line had vanished by 1900.

Cattal station nearly thirty years later, with an updated lighting system, better fencing, no telegraph posts and double glazing which has taken away the quarter lights. There are less chimney pots, but a seat to sit on.

C.T. Goode.

Cattal station looking east.   *C.T. Goode.*

    The pattern of lines is now becoming clearer, with the NER obtaining powers for a line from Knaresborough to Boroughbridge, which did in fact encounter competition from another, cheaper promoter whom the latter town actually preferred to carry out the work; however the NER won, obtaining extra time and powers enabling them to begin work in July 1870 and look around for likely contractors. Work seemed to progress at a leisurely pace. On 14th. October 1873 a navvy was killed and two injured when 17 ballast wagons ran away and were derailed.

    The line between Church Fenton and Wetherby was never developed to any great degree, except for a period during World War Two at Thorpe Arch, and Sturton station near Tadcaster was closed in 1905. Between 1925 and 1928 the route was used by the Harrogate Pullman, forerunner of the Queen of Scots. At Thorpe Arch (Wetherby) a munitions factory was set up in 1942, with its own railway and stations serving a large work force. A branch from Crossgates on the Leeds & Selby was opened to Wetherby. Single at first, it was doubled in 1902 with improved connections at Wetherby allowing through running between Leeds and Harrogate, so that Newcastle trains could enter Leeds from the east instead of the west and avoid reversal, running on to Liverpool quite easily. The heavy gradients proved a hindrance, though the line was again used for a time in diesel days. An improved station was built at Wetherby on the alignment of the new line.

Once the coal depot at Brunswick had closed, the business was transferred to Starbeck which, as may be deduced, was quite an important centre for traffic. In the early days there was an engine shed at Knaresborough which survived until about 1875. Starbeck acquired one in due course, in 1858 when the South yard expanded along with the traffic. Many through goods workings passed through between the West Riding and Teesside, some 85 movements daily in 1882, as well as 35 passenger trains. In 1893 a coal strike by West Riding miners created a high demand for Durham coal, and protests arose locally over the whistling of passing trains as they indicated which route they wished to take. This led to bell keys being placed on the east wall of the loco. shed, to tell the signalman at Starbeck South which line was required. Similar was set up in Harrogate North box at the station. By 1908 some 510 men were employed at Starbeck, which caused an increase in population from 800 in 1889 to 5,000 in 1909. In 1898 Starbeck station was extended and a new roof provided.

In 1862 a goods yard was opened in Harrogate opposite Oxford Street, but the site was deemed to be too noisy for the locals. The traffic went therefore to Starbeck until 1898 when a yard in Bower Road was opened, close by the station. Harrogate seems to have been just as wayward about its passenger facilities. There was a long platform alongside the main buildings, to which all trains came and went. A sort of platform had existed on the east side from 1866, connected up but unsurfaced and without a footbridge.

Royal visitors were brought to the town side of the station, so the company wished to let its senior and more fragile clientele be pampered in this way. By 1873 a footbridge was provided at the south end and a surface was installed. True relief came to the east side in 1898 when the platform was extended, presumably roofed, beneath the Station bridge and taking in two bays at the south end. The footbridge was relocated in the centre and the eastern approach to the station came in at right angles instead of alongside. Strange it is that, today, Harrogate station seems to have kept the same habit of using only its west platform whenever possible, leaving the eastern side virtually unused and uncovered apart from a bus shelter. No doubt the fragile and senior denizens are still grateful.

Incidentally the old Brunswick tunnel was prepared as an air raid shelter for up to 5,000 people during 1938.

Belmont signalbox with occupant. *C.T. Goode.*

4. The East & West Yorkshire Junction Railway.

To come more closely to the subject of this work, which turns out to be a very pleasant and modest branch line, with main line overtones, which has survived more or less since its opening to the east of Knaresborough on 30th. October 1848 with its nine stations intact, though four were to close on 13th. September 1958. Even so, the remainder are a close-knit and pretty bunch and attract for the line a fair tally of passengers on the hourly service of diesel units since, in most cases the villages they serve are close and paradoxically the line follows closely the route of the busy road which deters some from taking the car. The hourly bus service is also much slower. If we consider the 20½ mile run of the line from York to Harrogate, we find that it was built in three stages over 14 years, the first stretch, as mentioned above, to Knaresborough from York called the E & WY JcR. This was a small company which was successful in gaining powers from Parliament in 1845, granted a year later. There was willing support from George Hudson who granted the use of York station and thus saved the expense of a separate terminus. At the other end of the line the Leeds & Thirsk made an offer of amalgamation with the line for which it obtained an Act. It was later discovered in October 1848 that the L & Th was edging out of this arrangement, so that the E & WR Jc. began negotiations once more with Hudson, always eager to go pot-hunting, so that it was arranged that the GN of E would take over operation of the line.

From Knaresborough the line could not proceed for three years, due to haggling firstly with the GN of E, then with its own directors from Leeds. Lastly, on 1st. July 1851 the line came under the aegis of the Y & NM, also owned by Hudson, this latter contract lasting for 99 years. So the L & Th opposition was scuppered and in 1852 the E & WR Jc. lost its old identity. Delay at Knaresborough had been caused by collapse of the stone viaduct over the Nidd, perhaps the best feature of the town. This happened just prior to completion on 11th. March 1851. Within three years a second crossing was made and the branch was extended through a tunnel into the station and over the viaduct to make an end-on connection with a short stretch of line from Starbeck opened, as often seemed to be the case at this time, on the same day, 1st. October 1851. The last stretch was built by the Leeds & Thirsk and through powers granted on 16th July 1849, since when the company had been re-formed as the Leeds Northern. For the short run to Harrogate passengers had to change on to unsatisfactory road omnibuses.

By now the idea of a 'branch' from York might be becoming somewhat strained, especially as nowadays the regular service runs through from Leeds to York and back. However, the original aim of the pioneers was Harrogate, so that is where one must head for.

An old 1914 view of Starbeck station, showing the tie-bars across the platforms.   *Lens of Sutton.*

Starbeck South signalbox survives.   *C.T. Goode.*

There was the Leeds Northern which came through Bramhope tunnel and ran to Thirsk, originally avoiding both Starbeck and Harrogate. In 1859 work began on a loop from near Starbeck south through Harrogate town to near the south end of the Brunswick tunnel and also by way of the connection from Pannal up, round and over the Crimple viaduct to permit working through Harrogate. Soon afterwards a mile long loop was put from Starbeck to Dragon Jc. and the connection and new station were opened on 1st. August 1862, though delayed by the problem mentioned earlier on p. 16.

The Report of the Commissioners of Railways for 1849 offers some well chosen final words here on the efforts of the Leeds Northern:

> 'The Leeds & Thirsk Railway (as it was) enriched the North of England with some remarkable engineering works - the Bramhope tunnel, cut through shale and sandstone, 3,763 yd. in length, 25 ft. in width and 25 ft. in height from the

23

foundation level, with four ventilation shafts 40ft. by 30 ft. external diameter, and the great stone viaducts over the valleys of the Aire, Wharfe, Crimple and Nidd, consisting respectively of 23, 21,10 and 7 arches, the span of the Aire being, with one exception 48 ft. each, of those over the Wharfe 60 ft. and those over the Crimple valley and Nidd 50 ft. In addition to these works there were two smaller tunnels 70 and 100 yd. long, a timber viaduct of 14 openings over the Ure (Ripon), embankments 47, 51, 60, 61 and 70 ft. high and cuttings 47, 49, 60 and 126 ft. deep. Some of the gradients were heavy, averaging for a distance of 3¾ miles chiefly between Headingley and Horsforth 1 in 100 and for a distance of 3 miles between Horsforth and Arthington (through Bramhope) 1 in 94. The Engineer of the line was Thomas Grainger of Edinburgh.'

Starbeck today is certainly cleaner, if nothing else.
C.T. Goode.

5 The line described - Poppleton Jc. to Hammerton.

Beginning at the York end of the branch, the line leaves the East Coast main line 1¾ miles north of the city at Poppleton Jc., renamed Skelton in 1938 and the end of the original resignalling of York station in 1951. The cabin was one of the NER's vast ones to the east side of the line and one which survived into the seventies. South of this was Clifton signal box on the same side which controlled entry and exit to the main goods lines on the west side. To the east was the paraphernalia of the York water treatment works. Once clear of the exit of several sidings, the main goods lines became the up and down slow lines, from which the double Harrogate lines diverged at Skelton Jc. By use of a ladder of points Harrogate traffic might also be taken to or from the fast lines at this point. The ladder system, which does away with rail crossings and resultant wear and tear on rail ends, and is common nowadays, was quite advanced practice for the LNER, and quite 'daring', as it required a train to travel, albeit a short distance, in the wrong running direction.

The line curves round to the west, which will be its main direction for some distance, with the railway engineer's yard occupying the space left by its parting from the main line. This yard of fair size, was connected to the down slow by a facing connection. To the left, the tails of some of the marshalling yard sidings come round also, but do not join the branch. It was always apparently easy for York branch trains to join the main line, as today when the light dmus can nip in between the main line workings for the short run-in.

Once clear of the junction and the line is on more or less level terrain in the Vale of York, with a first halt at Poppleton (1m. 440yd. from the last signal box). It is pleasant to comment on the fact that, today the stations are probably prettier and more attractive than ever they were, and Poppleton draws favourable comments from passengers.

Good modelling material. Knaresborough station from above the tunnel. The viaduct is hardly visible beyond.
C.T. Goode.

The villages of Upper and Nether Poppleton are both large and lie on each side of a loosely drawn square of roads to the north of the station, close by, which is at the level crossing on the road leading to the A59 crossing the line nearby on what was once a tricky, skew overbridge. The platforms are parallel and the station building is set on the north side, a charming combination of two storey building in neat brick, set gable-end to the track, with stone quoins on the corners and flanking two storey additions on each side, these having their lower rooflines parallel to the platform. Pride of place is a bay window at ground level, set centrally. At some stage a glass canopy was added, carried on six light iron pillars running the length of the building. The level crossing is controlled by a wooden signal box set on the north side. Opposite this at present on the south side is land used intensively by a local garden centre which, rather intriguingly operates a 2 ft. gauge system of mining style tipper wagons to transport internal loads around. There was a long siding on the south side which ran behind the platform where a coal drop was situated along with a weighing machine, the siding unusually crossing the road at the level crossing along with the running lines, beyond which it joined them by a trailing connection, leaving a long headshunt. There was a main-to-main crossover by the signal box. Poppleton was favoured for many years as being the only other stop on the line for certain trains, excepting the usual stops at Knaresborough and Starbeck. For a time rail buses would make a return trip to Poppleton at breakfast time, most likely either for railway office staff or schoolchildren who lived there.

Knaresborough signal box. *C.T. Goode.*

Knaresborough station and the tunnel.   *C.T. Goode.*

    Poppleton to Hammerton was the first section of line which was singled some 25 years ago, between which was the first of the closed stations at Hessay, (2,585yd.) where the small village was about half a mile away to the south, while to the north there would be little to generate traffic, merely the A59. Hessay station is still very much in evidence, of greyish bricks but still with the stone quoins, a two storeyied gable and facing the station but with a low single storey building attached at the York end. Again the building is on the northerly of the two parallel platforms with the single line passing what remains of the southerly one. As at Poppleton the gates are worked by hand and controlled and signalled from a frame outside on the platform. To the west is a set of four sidings and a line serving the premises of an ex Army military stores depot; the outlet to the down line is controlled by a frame released by Hessay, plus a crossover. At the present time the sidings are disused and the depot is to let as industrial units. Originally there was a signal box to the west of the level crossing on the north side. The station was not popular in the timetable for all its life, often the first to be missed out by stopping trains.

A three car 'pacer' unit crosses Knaresborough viaduct, the view taken from the castle.   *C.T. Goode.*

    The second closed station on the line is Marston Moor (1,438 yd.), the name probably seized upon by the railway company as an early tourist 'crowd puller', though the site of the battlefield of 1644 is a good two miles south of here, with Long Marston village even further. Again, there is nothing to the north but the A59, a Roman road by the way. Cromwell's troops won the day, so it is perhaps the ghosts of the defeated Royalists who troop on parade to the station to seek the name of the place where they were slaughtered. The building is well maintained and is exactly the same in appearance as Poppleton, even to having had the glass canopy at one time. The small signal cabin governs the hand operated gates of the crossing from the west side, while to the south behind platform, both parallel, was at one time the coal depot and loading dock on a single siding, with a short siding on the north side. It is a surprise why such a relatively well equipped station with a fair range of goods facilities was ever built at such an isolated spot. Beyond, the line encounters the rather feeble and tortuously meandering river Nidd, reluctantly running to meet the Ouse at

Beningborough. This is crossed by an iron bridge just at the level crossing at Wilstrop Siding (1m.852yd.), where there was a short siding on the down side running into a shed with open sides, presenting a ramshackle appearance, especially in the company of Marston Moor's distant signal which was of venerable NER vintage. Both lasted into the seventies. For a long time up to May 1931 a train would stop on Saturday morning to take up passengers for York, while an afternoon train would drop them off later. This assumes that some sort of platform would be provided here for each direction, though older maps do not make this clear. Again the clientele would be thin on the ground, with Skip Bridge farm to the north and, away to the south Wilstrop Hall and Grange. The siding was worked by a frame released by key from the gatehouse.

The gradient up to Harrogate from Dragon Jc. Harrogate North signalbox just visible on the right.   C.T. Goode.

Hammerton station (1m.355yd.), 8¾ miles from York is encountered next and is approached on a slight embankment as the line turns fully westwards. Here the single line becomes double for the run to Cattal (1m.857yd), the stretch making a convenient passing place for present day services. An interesting point here is that the run of posts and insulators has been left in position along the north side of the line at the time of writing. Remarkable also, is that the station building, like all the others, is on the north side of the line - possibly the architect wished to give the staff the sunniest aspect on winter days, but here the building is not as cohesive as the ones met earlier. Here a tall, two storey house by the road, which lacks windows of any size, is flanked by a single storey building gable-end to the platform. This in turn is flanked by a wooden lean-to canopy to a brick structure, in the centre of which the signal lever frame is set behind what looks at first sight like a Victorian fire screen. Why this apparatus is not set next to the crossing either open or covered is not clear, as the operator has a longer walk to take the single line tablet to the driver of a train or collect it, as well as handling the crossing gates. To the east of the station on the north side was a short siding serving the small dock and weighing machine, with a main to main crossover between the platforms. Across the road to the north was the Station Hotel. Beyond this and across the A59 is the village of Green Hammerton at the junction with the Boroughbridge road, while to the south and close by is Kirk Hammerton, both large places and, since the A59 has now by-passed Green Hammerton, the latter is now expanding with new housing for commuters. Hammerton was important enough in the past for Bradshaw to include Hammerton as the only intermediate station on its heading for the line's timetable, between York and Knaresborough.

6 The line described - Cattal to Goldsborough.

As mentioned Cattal is at the other end of the double line section and is furnished with a respectable wooden signal box at the west end of the station by the road on the north side, similar in style to the box at Marston Moor. Like the latter place the station serves nowhere in particular, with Cattal village 1¼ miles to the south and Whixley 1½ miles beyond the ever present A59. From Hammerton the line has been in shallow cutting for a change, and reaches probably the best goods facilities on the branch with coal drops at a siding on the south side connected across to the running line on the north side, while on this side is a decent yard of four sidings, one long one and one running through a goods shed, the only surviving one on the line. The Victoria Inn is handily placed by the station, while on the road to the south was a maltkiln, unconnected to the railway. A vast tract of sloping land to the north of the station was, and

The unprepossessing west, or main platform at Harrogate.
C.T. Goode.

The lean-to that was Harrogate South. C.T. Goode.

still is, occupied by a market garden. The station is a hotchpotch of different shapes and sizes of building, four in all in the Poppleton style with the end gable of the two storey building, then a single storey structure parallel to the platform linked to another end-gable half-timbered style finished off at the end by a touch of Dutch hipped roof. Originally the station buildings were united by a glass canopy in the style of Poppleton. It would be very interesting to know why such lavish facilities were provided here; possibly it was to encourage development locally, if thoughts turned in such directions 160 years ago, and one wonders how much traffic would in fact be generated. The present single line resumes here.

Today's Harrogate, looking towards Leeds.   C.T. Goode.

The final two country stations, Allerton and Goldsborough were the third and fourth closed earlier in September 1958, and it is easy to see why, in view of their isolation. Allerton was distinguished by being at the level crossing with the A1 main road, and its gates, which were latterly very decrepit, could cause long traffic hold-ups for the road as a D49 would slowly draw into the station with a three coach stopper. Surely the signalman would not be required to appear and work these gates by hand? This was the only station on the line which had staggered platforms, so that a driver could draw up with his train clear of the crossing, allowing the gates to be reopened quickly, an essential procedure at Allerton. The station building, which was a standard gatekeeper's premises plus bay window end-on to the line, was flanked by a single storey structure which took care of the few passengers. Earlier, this had had a glass canopy and a low platform in front, probably the original set-up as found also at Howden and Hemingbrough. The crossing signal box was to the east, with the later platform and minimal wooden shelter beyond. Opposite the main building was the south platform, also minimally clad. On the north side at the west end was a two road yard serving coal drops, with a crane in attendance, together with a weighing machine. A crossover in the running lines was installed. The nearest habitation was New Inn farm close by. A little further to the north is the grand estate of Allerton Mauleverer, the mock gothic house only as old as the line itself. Probably as a nod towards possible custom from that source, the name of Allerton was used for the station - none of the luxury architecture of Castle Howard station here - but eventually they succumbed, having probably had confusion in passengers' minds with Allerton (Bywater) or Allerton (Liverpool) and looked round for a suitable option, quite a task though the lot fell on Hopperton, a hamlet vaguely linked by footpath a mile or so away. The change of name came on 1st October 1925.

Starbeck shed on the last day of service. Visible are Nos. 64861, 62759, 'The Craven', 62738 'The Zetland' and 67462. *Photo: N. Stead.*

D49 No. 62727 'The Quorn' visits with a Leeds stopping train at Harrogate. C.T. Goode.

Every station tells a story, and Goldsborough's is different (1m.1,043yd.). The line has now turned north west to run for a mile or so on noticeably rising gradients before turning due west again to arrive at Goldsborough at the same time as the A59 which crossed the line from the north, making an awkward turn to the west beyond the railway. However, a smart, new by-pass straightened out matters here, taking the road across the line by quite a graceful bridge. More recently, radical widening of the A1 and an interchange with the A59 caused, as well as the widening, a second bridge to appear alongside the A1's original bridge over the line at Hopperton; the station building here survives by a whisker. There was a long siding on the south side which ran behind the platform, where there was a coal drop and weighing machine, the siding unusually crossing the roadway with the running lines, beyond which it joined them by a trailing connection leaving a long headshunt. A crossover linked the running lines at the signal box. The platforms were staggered, though counter to the correct practice as at Hopperton, so that stopping trains would be likely to halt with the engine planted across the crossing in each direction. The yard, of two lines to the south opposite the north platforms was easily reached from the roadway. The down home signal was a feature bracketed out from the wrong side of the line, possibly because of the curvature of the site. During the 1939-45 war a cold storage depot was built to the west of the station on the north side, served by rail and including two long sidings. After the war the premises were taken over by the local Co-op for use as a bacon factory, while today's use is not readily obvious. For a time the sidings were used for the storage of spare wagons and brake vans. When the extra set-up appeared, the old signal box or frame was replaced on the same spot on 10th. November 1942 by a hideous 'modern' brick building to clash dreadfully especially as the station has a good set of fancy barge boards. The height of the line is now 136ft. above sea level.

Class D21 4-4-0 No.2140.   *Colling Turner Photos*

Ltd. Goldsborough has a high sounding name for a pleasantly rolling piece of countryside, with the village set one mile to the south of the line and road, with the Hall and its estate still further to the south, abutting on to Ribston Park and Hall. The Nidd, still full of meanders, bounds the perimeter of all this as it leaves the Knaresborough gorge. The presence of nobility might lead one to have expected a better class of station, but no, the building, still on the north like all the others, has a station house gable end-on with a crude single storey block structure on its flank on the west side.

The surprise item about Goldsborough station, in view of what has just been stated, will please the reader. When Princess Mary, late the Princess Royal, married in 1922 she lived firstly at Goldsborough Hall and then at Harewood House nearby, and was often visited by her mother, the Queen Mary. In 1923 King George V and the young Duke of Kent travelled to Goldsborough station for a christening at the local church. The train used was the LNWR Royal set of ten coaches brought from York by an LNER engine painted black, presumably to match the rolling stock. At Goldsborough two ex Midland locomotives, probably 'Compounds' were attached for the return journey to York and St. Pancras, and were joined by the Queen who had arrived independently by road. Having no doubt caused massive disruption at this little station, firstly to local train services and chaos over the level crossing of the A1, other means of conveying the royal personages other than by a full blown royal train were tried. Thus, in 1924 the King and Queen went to Harrogate by rail in a royal saloon attached to the "Harrogate Pullman" and motored to the Hall, the Queen leaving Goldsborough in the royal saloon attached to a Harrogate-York passenger train. The rest is perhaps worth the telling:

Allerton (Hopperton) was more of a Plain Jane than Goldsborough and the building stands on the low, unused platform from which the cover photo was taken facing right.
Photo: K. Hoole Trust

Goldsborough. A pretty station building with pretty barge boards, ruined by the presence of the brick signal box. The yard entrance is in the foreground. Photo: K. Taylor. 1970

In August 1927 the Queen arrived at Harrogate in a royal saloon attached to the "Harrogate Pullman" which had run non-stop from King's Cross headed by Class A1 No.2561 "Minoru". The King and Queen came to Harrogate on 21st August 1933 in a nine coach royal train, whereafter followed yearly visits by the Queen to Harrogate in a royal saloon attached to the 1.40pm. from King's Cross, arriving at 6pm. via Church Fenton, the final stretch being double headed by a D49 and older NER D Class engine. No problem with the Queen's weight here, merely the gradients. This happened in successive years to 1936 when the Queen returned to London in the saloon attached to the 'Yorkshire Pullman' which ran over the Starbeck-Pannal 'old' line instead of via Crimple Jc. On 12th. September 1938 the Queen arrived from Scotland with the saloon attached to the 'Queen of Scots' which, headed by an A4 No.2511 'Silver King' used the 'wrong' platform at Harrogate. The Monarch left Harrogate on 19th September 1938 on the 'Yorkshire Pullman' headed by A4 No.4498 'Sir Nigel Gresley' which took its usual route via York, leaving Harrogate at 11.15am. and taking 27 min. non-stop over the branch. No mere branch, this one!

D20 No.1206, possibly at York shed.

Colling Turner Photos Ltd.

7 Knaresborough - Environs and history.

A short cutting and longer embankment are met with on the way westwards before the outskirts of Knaresborough are reached, with climbs at 1 in 190 through Goldsborough and 1 in 127/119 and 152 into Knaresborough. Approaching Knaresborough the line, now on high embankment bears left through smallholdings and soon met up with the branch from Boroughbridge and Pilmoor, the single line running in from the right to join at Knaresborough Goods signalbox to the north of the line. The junction with the branch was double for a short way, indeed, about 1909 the branch was double towards Copgrove, the first station thereon. The goods sidings were supervised by the junction signalbox and were in a cramped location, with two lines to a coal depot on the north side and three short sidings to a dock and goods shed, with a long headshunt for a run-back into a saw mill. Here there was a travelling crane to lend some importance to the site. Actually the whole area had a decrepit look about it, not helped by being out of the sun, deep in a square sided cutting and equipped with some rather antiquated signalling. There appeared to be three running line crossovers, one on the Boroughbridge line, one outside the signal box and a slip as part of the siding entry just before the tunnel.

A short run through this tunnel to enter Knaresborough and a different world. Here is a small but very interesting town of 13,000 people which stands in marked contrast to Harrogate, the tourists' town (ask any knowledgeable group of foreigners), with a proper market place, a town crier, plenty of small shops and a genuine castle. The latter occupied the top of a sandstone edge overlooking the Nidd at a bend where the 70ft. high viaduct takes our railway across at about 50ft. lower than where the viewer stands, probably lending more dominance to the structure, with its seven arches, than is really the case. Rough days have been marked down in the town's history. In 1318 the Scots, on one of their forays into Yorkshire, attacked St. John's

Church below the station to the north of the town, where the residents were in hiding. Eventually the intruders fled after attempting to burn the place down. The Church, restored in 1870, is home to the remains of the Slingsby family, housing the tomb of Sir Henry Slingsby (1600), thereby stealing a march on Harrogate as he was the person who discovered the first medicinal well in that town. The castle remains are spread over 2½ acres and included the Keep, well preserved, and date from the presentation of the structure by Edward III to John of Gaunt (c.1350). The castle was under siege from the Roundheads in 1644 and was dismantled four years later.

Visitor. Class 4F No. 43906 probably on a return trip home with an excursion, waits at the west platform at Harrogate in May 1956. The detail is interesting, including the signal arm on the horizontal bar above the first coach, and low-tech stopping device in the foreground.   Photo: N. Stead Coll.

A quieter life may be found down by the river (for a small fee) to find a wall of limestone through which a spring falls into recesses and caves, causing lime deposits to form on objects which over the years have been hung in the water to form petrified specimens. Legend has it that Mother Shipton, daughter of the devil, dwelt nearby. Did we say 'a quieter life?'

'Near to the famous dropping well
She first drew breath as records tell.
And had good beer and ale to sell
As ever tongue was tipt on.
Her dropping well itself is seen
Quaint goblins hover round their queen
And little fairies tend the green
Call'd forth by Mother Shipton.'

(Poem carved on the wall of the inn nearby.)

Knaresborough station (2m.1,591yd.) keeps a low profile and is a single storey structure of grey stone containing nine rooms of different sizes, longest forming an attractive apsidal end at the south west end next to a level crossing. The crossing comes as a surprise, placed between a tunnel and the viaduct, with the station signalbox whose only other job is to work a crossover, close up to it. This a squarish brick building angled outwards on the track side and taller than it is long, decidedly a one-off. Currently the post is retained at the end of the single line section and to supervise the turn-round of units back to Leeds. The platforms are nicely canopied over the length of the buildings on each side and the mouth of the tunnel is decorated. At the entrance was a large NER pattern bracket signal carrying the down starter above the distant for the Goods signalbox beyond. A climb up the nearby lane to a spot over the tunnel will reveal a worthwhile view of the whole scene, good inspiration for a model railway layout.

8. Starbeck and Harrogate.

The line had become double as it passed the site of the goods yard and remains so through the station and out over the viaduct. Views from viaducts are never as interesting as the structures themselves seen from ground level. Progress is made through a shallow cutting past a new golf course on the north side before reaching Belmont Crossing, the signalbox of wood with its gable-end to the line on the south side; here for a short time a spur ran off southwards forming one side of a triangle to the Leeds Northern main line, enabling traffic to avoid the busy yard area at Starbeck. Our line swings round to the north west to enter Starbeck station past the level crossing of the High Street at Starbeck South (1m.1,087yd.) now the only remaining signal box hereabouts, which brings our branch into the Leeds Northern line for a time. In the triangle formed was the extended engine shed of two roads, turntable and several sidings, while facing south were fifteen sidings joining at the south point of the triangle at Stonefall signalbox. From here two reception roads ran from the northbound line up to Starbeck South, with eight long attendant goods lines and various shorter lines all coming together next to a maltkiln and the Station Hotel. Still in this part of town, to the east of this activity was Spa Mews down Spa Lane with its little park, bowling green, a sulphur spring and laundry. All in all, then, railwaymen at this spot had a fine choice of intoxication or recuperation, or perhaps a mixture of both!

Starbeck station was a no-nonsense affair, just north of the level crossing with the main, single storey building on the north side, of true NER suburban construction. Opposite was the complementary curtain wall backing the platform and both sides were fully canopied, and, unusually, braced across by nine girders at intervals. There was a pedestrian subway beneath the road. This was Starbeck station at its best, to be followed by a shortening of the platforms and smaller awnings with draught arresters at each end and, most recently, the dreaded bus shelter. A completely fitted out goods depot occupied the site in front of the station on the south west side, with easy road access. There were two weighing machines and, firstly, four roads serving a large goods shed, then eight roads served by a crane and beyond there four lines to a dock and two spare sidings. The whole funnelled in northwards to connections at Starbeck North (361yd.), where a headshunt led on to a factory siding. On the north east side things were less complicated, apart from a single down refuge siding. In the town nearby were two brickworks and a saw mill which were not rail linked, and a mineral water works.

A small 0.6.0 tank No. 68393 brings the rather heavy looking evening pick-up past the Air Ministry fuel siding north of Starbeck. The four tank wagons may well be detached here, the engine drawing forward with them and backing into the yard.   *Photo: N. Stead Coll.*

ENVIRONS OF HARROGATE AND KNARESBOROUGH

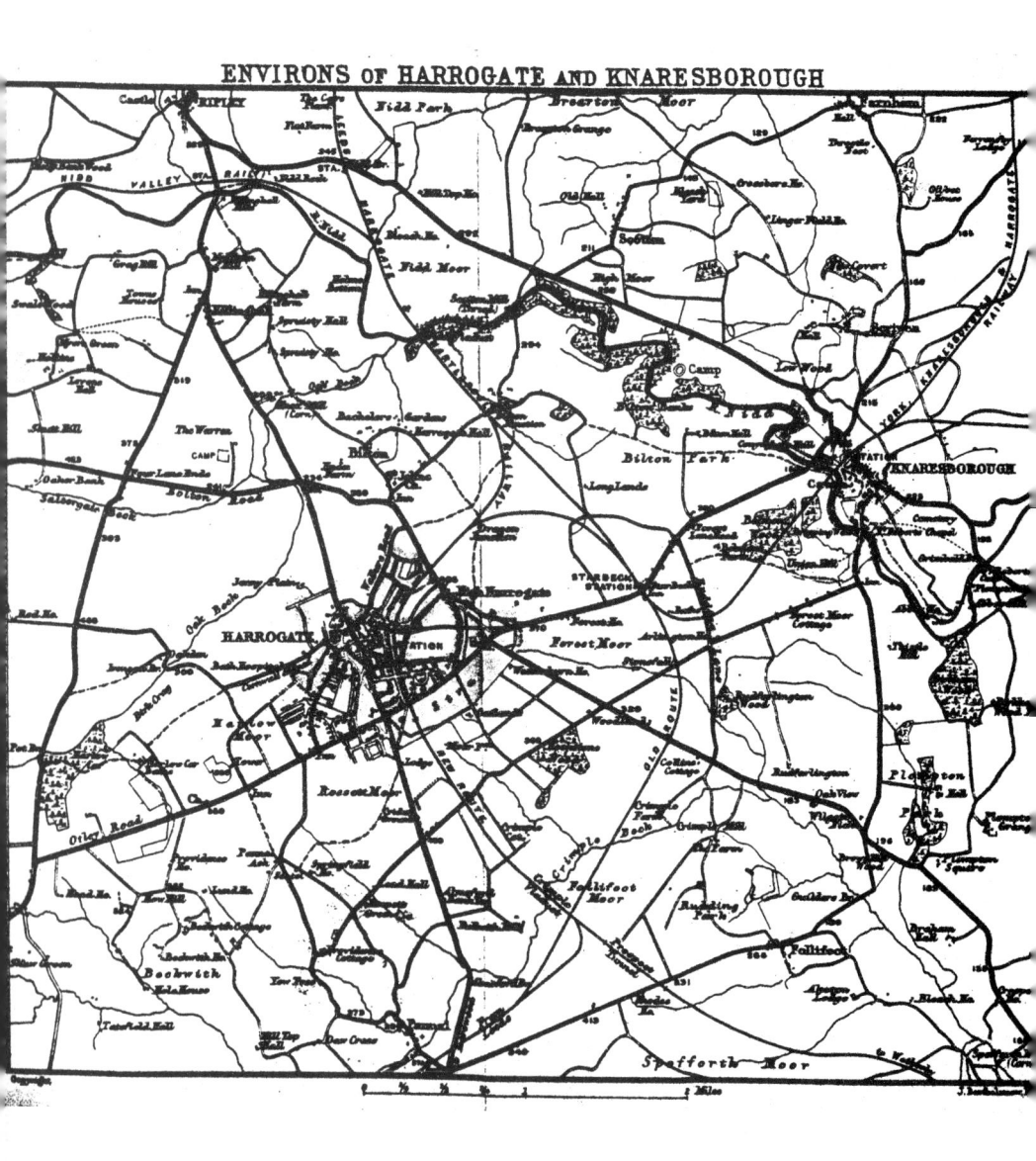

It is wise here to keep an eye on the accompanying map, to avoid confusion over which lines went where. At the North box the Leeds Northern went its way over the right hand fork, while our branch took a left turn over what became known as the Dragon Loop. The Leeds Northern had run straight up from Pannal through Starbeck from Leeds to Northallerton and the north from 1st. January 1856, going by way of Melmerby and Thirsk until 1901 when the Melmerby-Northallerton route was doubled and became more important. Thereafter the Thirsk branch declined, perhaps because the station at Thirsk was a long way out of the town centre, and was finally closed in 1959.

The Leeds Northern line from Pannal to Starbeck direct also declined, with only certain excursions, mainly Midland ones, using the line in order to enter Harrogate from the north to avoid taking the engine off for the return trip. The last workings were goods ones and the line closed in 1951, part of the formation becoming the Yorkshire showground.

Harrogate. Station forecourt in horse-drawn days, with not a trace of litter or manure. Photo: OPC Collection

The Dragon loop runs round on a wide curve to join the site of the Leeds Northern line from Harrogate to the north at Dragon Jc., now sadly no more. Halfway round was a petrol storage depot for the WD, situated on the north side. At Dragon a facing point took off a siding from the branch to run rather loosely behind the box and accompany the running lines up the stiff 1 in 64 into Harrogate. This rather eccentric line produced, firstly an extra companion as a sort of run-round loop, then singled again beneath the Skipton Road bridge, re-emerging as a double line once more, this time nearer to the main lines and becoming a nominal goods line as far a the station area. The 'companion' became three or so long sidings, after sending long spurs into the goods yard, some eleven in all, four of which terminated either in or alongside the goods shed. There were five cranes available for traffic and weighing machines near the road access from Bower Road.

Harrogate station looking north along Platform 4, from which a train for Leeds, headed by a G.N 4.4.0 is about to leave.
Photo: OPC Collection

Harrogate North signalbox (1,307yd. from Dragon) was a large affair on the west side, opposite the station turntable and supervising two goods lines on the east side, the up and down main lines to the Up and Down platforms with a through centre road northbound, though, surprisingly, only a siding occupied the space where a southbound road could have been placed. At the north end, west side were two bay lines; one line exists today, but is segregated from the station proper by a fence. Just north of these was a small yard of four lines for the storage of rolling stock. At this period in 1909 the station layout was perhaps at its largest, perhaps fussiest, covered by a vast amount of glass canopy. The forecourt, too, had an iron and glass porte-cochere.

Beyond the station bridge the tracks were brought into two again at Harrogate South, a lean-to affair which clung to the wall of the cutting behind it, on the west side. Within the station were a couple of gymnastic signals, one of which was slung beneath the canopy for east side departures, the other, possibly of later date, protruding out on a horizontal bar from beneath the western canopy to signal trains presumably wishing to run wrong line on the centre running road. There were two bays at the south end, each side at a fair distance from the main entrance over the footbridge.

Harrogate as a town has 64,000 inhabitants to Knaresborough's 13,000 and lived long on its reputation as a spa which fostered a luxury hotel trade. Today, the manufacturing trade fairs and conferences help things along, and to fill the remaining hotels. As the early guide book has it: 'the town is handsome but not picturesque.' The flower gardens are superb in season, the shops are fair though not outstanding, recently enlivened somewhat by a modest shopping centre near the station. The latter suffered an impersonal rebuilding several years ago, while the North signalbox was replaced by a lifeless modern brick structure, still with us, on the east side in 1946.

9. Passenger Services.

Anyone living at the halfway point on the line, say at Hammerton, had an easy choice of distractions from the outset, with Harrogate and Knaresborough to divert in one direction and York in the other. The earliest timetable which the author has been able to peruse is from the 1871 Bradshaw, which offered five services each way, leaving York at 7.10, 10.20am., 2.50, 4.35 and 7.20pm., and Harrogate at 8.35am., 12.10, 3.05, 4.30 and 7.00pm. All stopped at each station except Hessay, apparently the 'dunce' from the early days, being a request stop. On Saturdays passengers for York were collected by the 9.35 at Wilstrop Siding and were returned there off the 4.35pm. This arrangement is interesting and might mean that the gatekeeper's wife and family had some good contacts in head office at York. Trains used in later years below are shown thus: *.

There were two runs between Knaresborough and Harrogate at 11.15am. and 9.20pm. and no Sunday trains. The running time was 65 minutes.

In 1880 the local service between Knaresborough and Harrogate had livened up to four each way, with extras on Weds. and Sats. only for market days at Knaresborough and York respectively. There was also a later departure from Knaresborough at 11.10pm. Over the branch trains left York at 7.25, 10.15am., 3.33*, 5.00 and 7.25pm., with the same duration of running time, though the 5.00 was an express taking 40 minutes and stopping at Cattal only, for some reason, plus Knaresborough and Starbeck. In the other direction trains left at 8.25*am., 12.15, 4.35 and 7.35pm. Again, there was an Up express leaving Harrogate at 9.10am. and calling at Cattal and Knaresborough only, again taking 40 minutes.

Sentinel railcar 'Royal Forester' running along the East Coast main line near Langley. Several cars were stationed in the Southern area of the L.N.E.R., this particular one at Hitchin.   *Photo: E. Neve Coll.*

Matters had greatly improved by 1900, with 12 trains each way on the Knaresborough-Harrogate local service, probably now worked by push-and-pull sets. There were now eight services along the length of the line, including fast runners which left York at 5.50pm. to reach Harrogate at 6.17pm. and at 7.00pm. reaching Harrogate at 7.33pm., thus taking the businessman into account. From Harrogate things were not quite so nifty, with the 8.58am. missing out Goldsborough, Hammerton and Hessay, while the 8.05am. reached York in 50 minutes with a conditional stop at Knaresborough. Wilstrop calls on Sats. were with the 11.05am. from Harrogate and 3.22pm. from York.

Prior to the Great War in 1914 services were slightly unbalanced, with 9 trains from York but 11 from Harrogate. Poppleton now entered the field with a petrol rail motor leaving York at 8.57am. arr. Poppleton at 9.02am., then a turn-round at 9.07am. arr. York at 9.13am. The reasons for this could be several-trial running, staff training, keep-the-thing-out-of-the-station-at-a-busy-time; certainly it ran too late for a school run if such existed at that time, or did a local railway worthy dwell in the village? It was just one more branch movement for the signalman at Poppleton Jc. to have to fit in.

There was a Saturdays only out of York at 11.00am. which is not shown as a return run. The mystery deepens.

Poppleton must have been the flavour of the year at this time, as the 12.15pm. express from York halted there, next stop Knaresborough, while at 6.22pm. it shared the honours with Cattal as halts before Knaresborough. There were two other expresses from York, the 2.00pm. taking 32 minutes, and 5.15pm. taking just 30 minutes. Of the eleven from Harrogate five were expresses, at 8.25am., 9.18am., 1.13pm., 3.98pm. which was a Cattal only and the 6.03pm. All performed in 35 minutes or less. Wilstrop passengers used the 10.55am. to York and 3.17pm. return. The Knaresborough-Harrogate trains had a separate timetable.

LNER days came in 1923, and in 1924 the petrol rail motor No.2105Y was showing its face around York and district, as follows:

York	dep:	12.25pm.
Copmanthorpe	arr:	12.35
Copmanthorpe	dept:	12.50
York	arr:	1.00
York	dep:	1.05
Strensall	arr:	1.22
Strensall	dep:	1.30
York	arr:	1.47
York	dept:	2.30
Poppleton	arr:	2.38
Poppleton	dept:	2.48
York	arr:	2.56	All Sats. only.

On Saturdays from September 1924 the evening cycle was extended to include a 10.30pm. run from York to Poppleton, with an empty arrival back in York at 10.52pm. The car then left York at 10.57pm. for Alne, reached at 11.19pm. to connect with the last train to Easingwold, then returning empty to York, arriving at 11.45pm. This was in conjunction with a special day excursion rate of 1/11d (10p) from Easingwold to York at the time.

In 1925 the above car, No. 2105Y ran from York to Poppleton at 8.57am., returning to York at 9.07am. There was also still the Sat. working at 11.00am. from York which ran back empty.

Branch trains in 1925 were nine each way as follows:

From York:
 7.15, 10.25am., 12.15pm. MWFO XP, 12.45, 2.10 MWFO XP, 3.29*, 5.15 XP, 5.18, 6.25 (calling only at Poppleton and Cattal), 7.55 and 9.25 SO XP. The fastest trains took 32 min.

From Harrogate:
 7.55, 8.25 XP, 8.33, 10.58*am., 12.40pm., 1.06 MWFO XP, 3.25, 5.08, 6.10 MWFO XP,   8.05, 10.25 SO XP.

For many years up to 1939 Hessay was always a conditional stop for the service at 8.05pm. from Harrogate, or the service nearest to this time. The total run for stopping trains took 52 minutes.

1930 saw the same running time for stopping trains; there were eight trains to Harrogate, plus two expresses on Wednesdays and a later service on Saturdays which set down only at Hammerton, Cattal, Hopperton and Goldsborough. From Harrogate there were nine trains, six stoppers and three fast trains, the 8.25am. having a halt at Poppleton as the rail motor had temporarily flown. Wilstrop stops on Saturdays were almost at an end. In this year they were made by the 10.54am. to York and 5.18pm. to Harrogate.

The new 'Sentinel' steam railcars were making an impact on the Knaresborough-Harrogate service, with a special Sunday working based on Starbeck shed every half hour, beginning as follows:

Starbeck	dep:	2.14pm.
Harrogate	arr:	2.20pm.
Harrogate	dep:	2.30pm.
Knaresborough	arr.	2.39pm.
Knaresborough	dep:	2.45pm
Harrogate	arr:	2.56pm.
Harrogate	dep:	3.00pm. etc.

In 1938 services were in some ways at their best, though hopelessly unbalanced with ten trains to Harrogate but only six in the reverse direction.

To Harrogate:
7.10, 9.10 XP, 10.00am., 12.15 WSO XP, 12.40, 2.25 WSO XP, 3.40, 5.15 XP, 5.23, 6.25, 7.55, 9.35pm.

To York:
7.30, 8.25, 11.15am. (Yorkshire Pullman), 12.20, 1.15 WSO XP, 3.45, 5.19, 6.00 WSO XP, 6.10 SO XP, 8.15, 10.45 SO pm.

The last train from York had several conditional stops, while the 8.25am. halted at Poppleton. Marston Moor was conditional on the 3.45pm. from Harrogate, and left out by the next train at 5.19pm. For the revellers the 10.45pm SO service stopped conditionally at four stations.

The 'Yorkshire Pullman' had taken this route because of the introduction of a new service, The 'West Riding Limited' which left Leeds non-stop for King's Cross at 11.33am. and would have cramped the style of the older train, which had gained its final name in 1935. In 1938 the Harrogate portion left at 11.15am., of four cars, joining up at Doncaster with two cars from Hull and two which had come from Halifax via

Bradford and Wakefield. Normally the train was thus made up to eight vehicles, though at weekends was strengthened up to eleven or even twelve vehicles. With a 'Pacific' at the head this would be a sight worth seeing and hearing.

At last the branch had a Sunday service of 'Sentinel' railcars in their smart green and cream livery:

H.gate dep:	12.00pm.	1.30	2.45	7.17	8.47	9.52
York arr:	12.40	2.09	3.27	7.57	9.25	10.25
York dep:	1.15	2.30	4.10	5.40	8.15	9.52
H.gate arr:	1.56	3.11	4.51	6.17	8.56	10.33

It would appear that a Starbeck car could work all the first four return trips, leaving the last two for a Harrogate and York car together.

With another war looming, the railways were preparing for the worst, staff shortages and commandeering of rolling stock to use for the war effort. The timetables were trimmed to something more basic, and frills such as the Pullmans were mothballed or used for special wartime requirements. Throughout wartime two or three Pullman cars in drab livery were parked in an overgrown siding near Barnby Dun station, used it was rumoured, for hush-hush military meetings. In 1939 there were six trains from York and five from the other direction, including a Sats. only express from York at 2.45pm., and retaining the 8.25am. fast service from Harrogate, even to the stop it made at Poppleton, managing things in 30 minutes. There was no Sunday service.

In 1941, once wartime routine was established matters relaxed a little and there were now seven workings each way along the branch.

To Harrogate:
    7.10, 10.10 am., 12.45 SX, 12.55 SO, 1.10, 4.15, 5.25, 6.35 and 8.18pm.

Hessay was served by the first train and the mid-afternoon working.

To York:
7.30, 8.20 XP, 9.00am., 1.05, 3.30 XP, 5.00, 8.05pm.

Both the 8.20 and 3.30 had a Poppleton stop, the latter also calling conditionally at Marston Moor. The 8.20 could still reel off the run in 30 minutes.

War over at last in 1949 and British Railways takes over, with seven trains to Harrogate and six in the other direction, plus a Sats. only working each way. The times are roughly similar to the 1941 list in each case, give or take a few minutes. Hessay was still rationed for stops, and the 12.40pm. SO to Harrogate covered the run in 33 minutes. The timetable for 1951 was almost identical. 'An uplift in morale is noticeable wherever diesels have been introduced, and a more brisk and businesslike attitude to train services both on the platform and on the line is apparent'. This statement was made by Mr. F.L. Hick, Asst. Operating Officer of the NE Region in 1958, before a learned body. He mentioned in his paper the success of dieselisation schemes, chiefly that began in June 1954, when the very first, Bradford (Exchange). Harrogate and Knaresborough service was implemented. After four years of operation the takings were five times the amount of that taken in the last years of steam on that particular line, but patronage had dramatically increased, bringing more units to the Line. Initially, the joys of uninterrupted all-round views from the dmus brought in so many customers that steam trains had to replace the new rolling stock to convey them all - another of life's ironies. Timekeeping was much improved, as was reliability.

In 1960 ten dmu services left York, roughly at half past the hour, as the idea of a fixed time per hour had not yet been achieved. From Harrogate, after 7.3am., and 9.05, nine departures left at a quarter past the hour until 6.35pm., the last being 8.35pm. Dmus had first appeared on the branch on 19th. September 1958, with some steam workings for a time. Sunday services were re-introduced for the summer season after a long time, and not throughout the year until 1967. The ultimately unsuccessful Class 141 rail buses were used between Leeds and Harrogate from May 1984 with a half hour service, continuing to York on an hourly basis. Today an assortment of dmu types may be seen on the workings. Over the years the branch has been used for sundry excursions and diversions, with excursions from York to Blackpool and other west coast resorts via Skipton, and in the reverse direction from places such as Keighley to Scarborough and the like. The conference trade in Harrogate has generated special workings from time to time, as does the Great Yorkshire Show.

Freight traffic has always been light and there was a regular pick-up goods which left York North Yard at 1.30pm., returning from Harrogate Goods at 7.30pm. There were also two slow goods which ran at 8.20am. from York Yard North and 2.20pm. from Stonefall Sidings, Harrogate. Two others were booked to be operated as required, out from Harrogate and return from York. Parcels traffic was originally too heavy for the dmu's capacity and it was felt that a special was required. This left York at 7.00am., calling at Marston Moor (for some reason) and Knaresborough, and was latterly a steam turn. Possibly the gradients at the Harrogate end dictated this, as the dmus working on the Hull-Scarborough line, which was mostly level, could haul long wheel base vans when required.

Hopperton closed to goods in November 1962, Poppleton and Hessay in May 1964, though the military depot at the latter place continued to be served by rail for longer. The rest, including Knaresborough closed to goods in May 1965, though the cold storage depot at Goldsborough lasted a few more years. Starbeck station buildings were demolished in 1978, the goods facilities going in October 1980, Harrogate's buildings had been reconstructed beneath a block of offices in 1963-5; the goods yard closed in July

1984, the fuel depot closing at Starbeck a few weeks before. Harrogate South signalbox had closed in 1981.

An official photo. of petrol-electric motor No.3170 on test run, coming off the Harrogate line at Poppleton Jc. Originally built, with No. 3171 in 1903, the car began life running between Scarborough and Filey and was scrapped in April 1931 after running around the York area.   Photo: LNER

10. Motive Power.

It is not always easy to put a finger on the shed which supplied an engine for a particular working over the branch, especially as the line was always a through one at both ends. When dmus became the fashion, cyclic rosters grew and rolling stock would appear with crews from Darlington, Botanic Gardens (Hull), York and Leeds on their way round after quite lengthy circuits. To mention the simpler goods workings first; in the 1950s the B16 4-6-0, a Starbeck engine, would be rostered for the slow goods, while a York J27 would handle the pick-up goods. York depot was a large one with a good range of engines, some on trial, a variety of which would work from Harrogate. Starbeck, however, concerns us most, as it was in the front line of many activities around the branch The shed came into being in 1857, presumably where it always stood at Starbeck, the first reference was to Low Harrogate. On closure of Brunswick station the shed was to be lengthened for two further engines, to be extended again in 1877, plus eight cottages at a cost of £1,432. On a request by the Midland Railway for a temporary home for two of their engines, the shed was lengthened to 150ft. in March 1888 with refinements in the layout. Further developments took place in 1900-1 and a new roof, was installed after 1945, whereafter, in 1953 this was replaced and the total length shortened from 370ft. to 270ft. It would appear from the allocation lists that the branch was operated by G5 0-4-4Ts, as there were ten available. Also in 1923 were one D17, D20, and D21 4-4-0, two D22s and three D23s - plenty of venerable motive power to choose from, though some may have been stored. In 1933 the picture was much the same, plus an increase to six A7 4-6-2Ts from four in 1923; these were used for goods trips to and from the Leeds area through the Bramhope tunnel.

In 1923 Starbeck sent out thirteen engines each day for passenger train working to all local places, using the G5s and the elderly 4-4-0s for longer workings. The allocations of course varied. In 1939 no less than thirteen D20s were to be found at Starbeck. These were strong and reliable 4-4-0s, capable of much hard work and greatly superior to the older D17s and the like. Their LNER numbers for the pundit, were: 712, 1026, 1042, 1206, 1207, 1236, 1258, 1672, 2020, 2101, 2104, 2105 and 2107. No. 2020 had been on the shed since 1937 and was specially fettled to haul the 'Yorkshire Pullman' from Harrogate to Doncaster, returning on the 2.20pm. slow Doncaster-Leeds and the 5.30pm. Leeds City-Knaresborough, each day. With the D20s at this time were four D21s and eleven G5s, plus one steam railcar which worked between Harrogate and Knaresborough fourteen hours a day. The other car was worked partly by Starbeck and Leeds men. In the summer of 1939 three railcars worked between Harrogate and Knaresborough, with five trips to and from York on Suns. Before finishing remarks on the 'Sentinels', it might be of interest to record which vehicles came to Starbeck shed on a regular basis: (In this case names are of more interest than the numbers.)

In 1928 'True Briton' worked the Harrogate-Knaresborough service. 'Hark Forward' arrived in November 1928, soon to go to Stockton. In August 1929 'Emerald' arrived, with 'Norfolk' as companion in April 1930, the two being shedded there until the war years, joined by 'Surprise' to make a trio in 1934. After 1943 only 'Defiance' was noted at Starbeck; this car had originally gone to York in 1929 to replace the duties performed by petrol car No. 2105Y. The last railcar of all was 'Woodpecker', which arrived in 1945 and was scrapped in 1947. In 1932 one car worked the Harrogate-Knaresborough shuttle service all day; in actual fact the first car which had begun at 5.25am. retired to the shed around midday, to be replaced by the second until 10.55pm.

On Saturdays there were return trips Harrogate-Wetherby and Harrogate-Melmerby, by way of a change of scene. In the thirties a Working Men's club in Harrogate regularly went on a special outing to Bridlington, using one of the cars, quite a mileage. The problem posed is: which route did they take? The author's money goes on Wetherby, Church Fenton, Selby and Market Weighton, though there was always York, Market Weighton and Driffield, or even York, Seamer!

The D49s were to make their presence felt only belatedly on the York-Harrogate line, and it was with some surprise that I realised that it was not until 1947 that they appeared on passenger workings. However, they had come to the area when new in 1928, Gresley's new three cylinder 4-4-0 named after Shires and Hunts in the LNER region, with the running fox on each splasher along with the nameplate. The names were always an excellent advert., and are still today, even if some of the names given do not readily trot off the tongue. Though powerful, they were impressive rather than elegant and were soon known to the crews as rough riders. During the war years they found difficulties with anything over five coaches behind on stiff gradients, and it was practice to use a pilot engine or set off with another of the class in tandem, hardly economical. Thirteen came to the North Eastern area in 1929, six to York, seven to Neville Hill (Leeds). The practice was to cascade these engines to other sheds like Hull Botanic, as newer ones became available, so that allocation lists were somewhat fluid. In 1933 Neville Hill had nine engines, York nine, Heaton two and Botanic Gardens seven. Settlement came in May 1939 when it was decided to concentrate as many of the same class at as few sheds as possible; witness the D20s mentioned above. Thus Leeds had fifteen D49s, York ten, Gateshead eight, Scarborough five and Hull fifteen. There was very little change during World War II, and twenty six were still at the same sheds in 1946 as in 1939. In 1947 Starbeck received its first D49s, in October - Nos. 2726/52/3 'The Meynell', 'The Atherstone' and 'The Belvoir', and in December Nos. 2762/73 'The Fernie' and 'The South Durham'. They were joined by 'The Morpeth' No. 2768, the two cylinder rebuild of 1942 which had the appearance of a D11 class engine below the footplate. It came to a sticky end after an accident at the shed. The advent of the handy, all-purpose B1 4-6-0s which were appearing in large numbers was beginning to put paid to the use of the D49s, and in September 1959 the five Starbeck members and a similar number from Selby went to Hull Dairycoates. Perhaps wrongly, the allocation for Starbeck shed in 1954 is shown as 1 B16, 16 D49s, 12 J39s (which were really D49s with small six coupled wheels) and three J77s. The humiliation was to find themselves working coal trains of twenty wagons from Gascoigne Wood (Selby) to Scarborough after 1955. The last were scrapped on May Day 1961, Nos. 62711 and 62729 'Dumbartonshire' and 'Rutlandshire'.

Eventually to be completely overshadowed by the D49s, the D21s, were a more powerful version of the D20s, though not as successful as the larger class of sixty engines. Only ten D21s were built, with larger boilers and with frames and fireboxes as long as the 'Atlantics' which they were intended to assist on the heavier trains. The numbers ran in a block of 1237-46, and until the thirties they were most attractive engines in green livery at first with brass beading to the splashers. Although their main territory was the York-Leeds area, some engines did appear at Starbeck to work the Leeds service as below:

> 1923 Seven at York, two at Neville Hill and No.1242 at Starbeck.
> 1925 1241 additionally at Starbeck.
> 1931 1241/2 at Starbeck, the rest all at Neville Hill, where they remained.
> 1935 1245/6 now at Starbeck.
> 1945 1242/5, the last two of Class left Starbeck for Neville Hill. No.1245, the last survivor, withdrawn in January 1946.

11. TIMETABLES, PLANS AND RAILWAYANA

325 YORK, KNARESBOROUGH AND HARROGATE.

WEEKDAYS

Page		a.m.	a.m.	a.m.	a.m.	a.m.	a.m.	p.m.	p.m.	p.m.	p.m.	p.m.	p.m.	p.m.	p.m.	p.m.
68	Newcastle .... dep.	1F50			8	9 20	19 20		12 18	12 56	2 45		4 6	4 50	5 7	
	Darlington .... "	2 27	6 27		8 65	10 34	11 21		12 18	1 50	3 43		5 1	5 50	6 45	
			X		SO			X				E				SO
	YORK .... dep.	7 15	8 20	10	p.m.	12 15	12 45	2 10	2 27		3 23	5 15	5 18	6 25	7 59	9 25
	Poppleton	7 23	8 26	10		12 22	12 52		2 36		3 28	5 24		6 31	8 1	
	Hessay	7 28		10 31			12 57				3 33	5 28				B
	Marston Moor	7 31		10 36			1 6				3 36	5 32			8 8	
	Cattal	7 37		10 45			1 11				3 42	5 38		6 42	8 15	9H40
	Hopperton	7 43		10 50			1 16				3 47	5 43			8 20	
	Goldsborough	7 49		10 55			1 20				3 52	5 48			8 25	
	Knaresborough A ...	7 54		10 59			1 28				3 56	5 52		6 52	8 29	9 50
	Starbeck	8 3		11 6	12 37		1 34		2 32		4 4	6 6	5 37	7 1	8 36	
	HARROGATE .... arr.	8 15		11 20	12 46		1 40	2 42			4 16	6 12	5 47	7 8	8 42	10 0

| 55 328 | Darlington .... arr. | 10 3 | | | p.m. 39 | | p.m. 45 | | | | | | p.m. 8 37 | | 10 25 | |
| | Newcastle .... " | 11 | | | 2 23 | | 56 18 | 4 50 | | 5 40 | 6 39 | | 10 9 | | 11 29 | |

WEEKDAYS

Page		a.m.	a.m.	a.m.	a.m.	a.m.	a.m.	a.m.	a.m.	a.m.	p.m.	p.m.	p.m.	p.m.	p.m.	p.m.	p.m.	p.m.	p.m.	a.m.
68 330	Newcastle .... dep.				1 31	7 35	10K 10 1 0 1 1P 4		12 10					2 45		4K 17	7 15	
	Darlington .... "				6 27	8 33	10 24 10 34 12P 5		1 9					3 43		4 25	8 25	
			X				E	SO	SX		SO	SO				SO			SO	
	HARROGATE .... dep.	7 24	8 25		8 30	10 30	12 46		1 6		3 35			5 10 1035					
	Starbeck .... A	7 27			8 39	10 33	12 12 45 12	1 7	1 11		3 40			5 13	6 10	8 10	10 40	
	Knaresborough	7 34			8 43	10 41	12 50 19 56	1 13	1 15		3 45			5 18	6 18	8 15	10 45	
	Goldsborough	7 39		D	8 47	10 46	12 55	1 17			3 49			5 22		8 19		
	Hopperton	7 43			8 52	10 51	12 59	1 22			3 54			5 27		8 24		
	Cattal	7 48			8 57	10 56	1 4	1 27			3 59			5 31		8 28	10M 57	
	Marston Moor	7 52			9 1	11 1	1 9	1 32			4 3			5 36		8 33		
	Hessay	7 56			9 5	11 5	1 14	1 37			4 8			5 40		8 37		
	Poppleton	8 3		8 40	9 10	11 11	1 18	1 40			4 12			5 45		8 42		
	YORK .... arr.	8 17		8 48	9 24	11 24	1 32	1 56			4 27			6 0	6 42	8 57	1112	

| 56 | Darlington .... arr. | | | | 11 5 | 1 39 | | | | | 2 51 | | 4 25 | 5 40 | | 7 10 | | a.m. 3 7 |
| | Newcastle .... " | | | | 11 10 | 2 49 | | | | | 3 45 | | 5 34 | 6 39 | 8 19 10 | | 9 11 | |

A For complete service between Knaresborough and Harrogate, see page 326.
B Calls when required to set down.
C Calls when required.
D Calls at 8.33 a.m. when required to take up.
E Calls on Saturdays at Wilstrop Siding (between Hammerton and Marston Moor) for York Passengers.
F On Mondays leaves at 1.31 a.m.

G Passengers can arrive Darlington 1.59 p.m. and Newcastle 4.50 p.m. by Pullman Car Express (see page 539).
H Calls to set down only.
K Via Stockton.
L Until 18.h October inclusive leaves Newcastle 12.10 p.m. and Darlington 1.9 p.m. (Wednesdays and Thursdays excepted).
P Pullman Car Express (see page 539).
SO Saturdays only.   SX Saturdays excepted.
Y Rail Motor Bus.   One class only.

TABLE Z—LOCAL WHISTLES

Line No.	Signal Box at which Whistle to be given		Whistle
	Harrogate—		
	South	To or from No. 1 Bay Platform	1 short, 1 long
		To or from No. 2 Bay Platform	2 short
		To or from No. 3 Siding	3 short
		To or from Up Main line and Middle Road	1 crow, 2 short
		Down Main to Middle Road	2 long
	North	To or from Middle Road and Down Main	3 short
		To or from Middle Road and Long Siding	3 short, 1 long
		To or from Horse Dock and Down Main	4 short
		To or from Horse Dock and Long Siding	1 long, 4 short
20 contd.	**Harrogate contd.—** North continued	To or from Horse Dock and Down Siding	4 short, 1 long
		Up Main to No. 3 Bay line	3 long
		Up Main to No. 6 Bay line	2 long
		Up Main to No. 7 Bay line	2 long, 1 short
		Up Main to Middle Road	2 short, 1 long
		Back Siding to Turntable	1 long, 1 short
		To or from Long Siding and Up Main	2 short
		To or from Long Siding and No. 3 Bay	3 short, 2 long
	Dragon	To or from Starbeck and Harrogate Goods Yard	3 long
		To run round train, or for shunting purposes	1 crow
	Starbeck—		
	Stonefall	From Leeds on the Main line	1 long
		To No. 1 Down Reception line	2 long
		To No. 2 Down Reception line	3 long
		Engine Shed to Up Sidings	2 long, 1 short
	South	To Engine Shed or Turntable line	2 short, 1 long
		To indicate that engine has passed into Loco. Yard and is clear of trap points	1 long, 1 short
		To or from Weigh Siding and Main line	3 short
		To or from No. 1 Reception line to Down Main line	2 short
		To or from No. 2 Reception line to Down Main line	3 long
		To or from No. 2 Reception line to Malt Kiln Siding	1 short, 1 crow
	North	Warehouse Group of Sidings to No. 1 Shunting line	2 long, 1 short
		Coal Depot line to No. 2 Shunting line	1 long
		Coal Depot line to No. 1 Shunting line	1 long, 1 crow
		Goods Yard to No. 2 Shunting line	2 long
		Goods Yard to No. 1 Shunting line	2 long, 1 crow
		Cattle Dock to No. 2 Shunting line	1 short, 1 long
		Cattle Dock to No. 1 Shunting line	2 short, 1 crow
		Sidings to Down Main line	3 short, 1 long

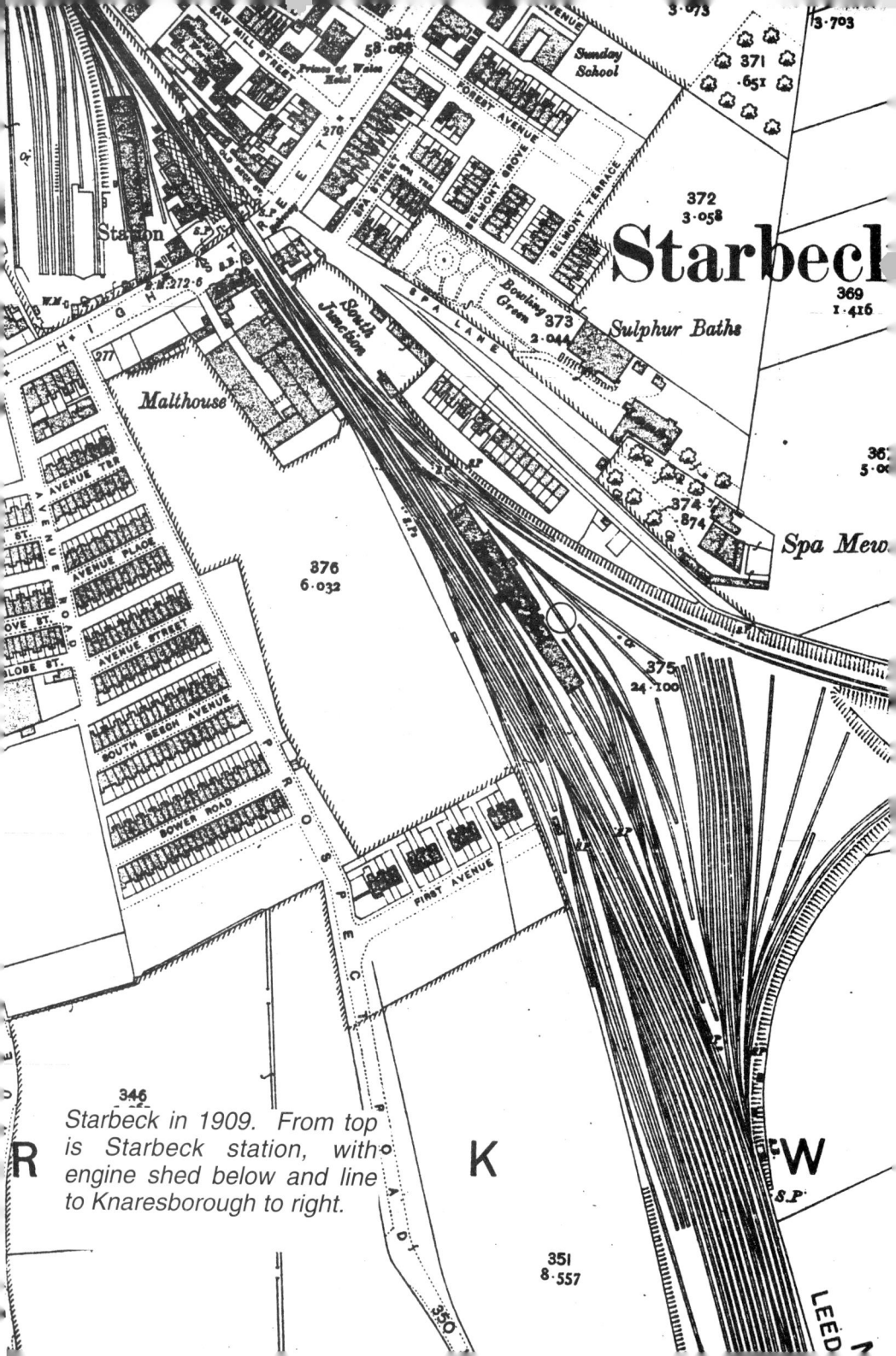

Starbeck in 1909. From top is Starbeck station, with engine shed below and line to Knaresborough to right.

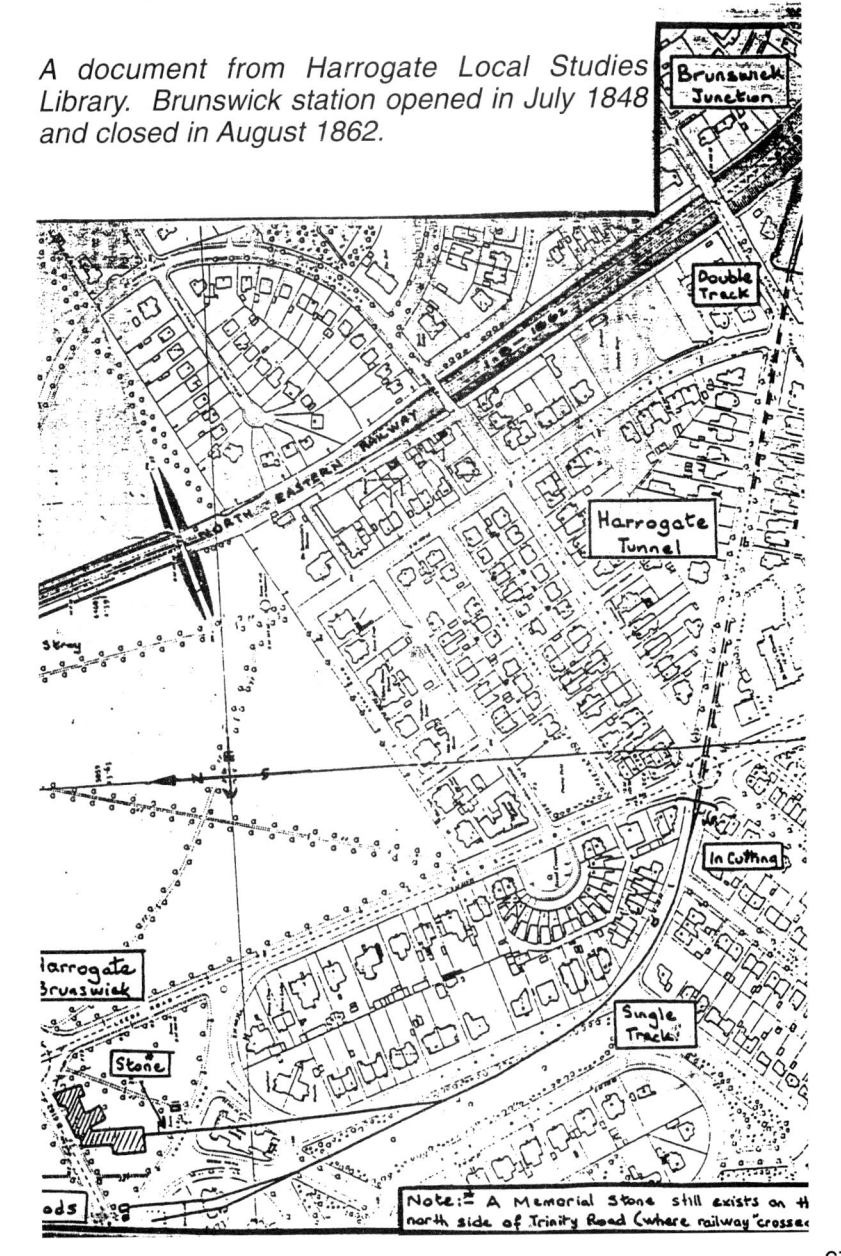

A document from Harrogate Local Studies Library. Brunswick station opened in July 1848 and closed in August 1862.

NEWCASTLE AND DARLINGTON JUNCTION RAILWAY.

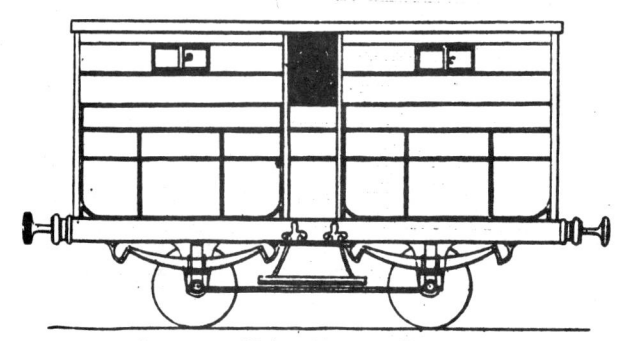

YORK AND NORTH MIDLAND RAILWAY.

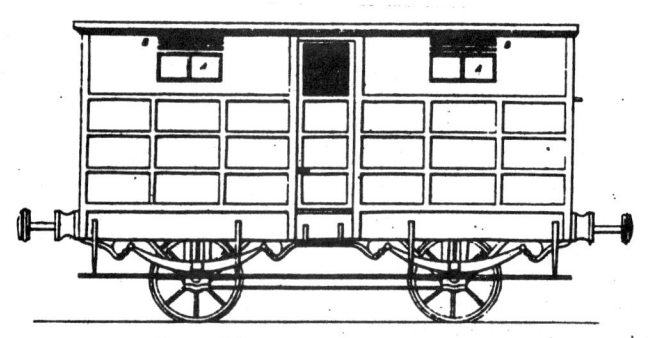

GREAT NORTH OF ENGLAND RAILWAY.
THIRD-CLASS CARRIAGES USED ON THE MAIN LINE IN 1845.
(TO SEAT 40 PASSENGERS EACH.)

Taken from a local newspaper of the day, c. 1926. The cars, decidedly primitive, were on loan from the Derwent Valley Light Railway, York. Photos taken at Knaresborough.

RAILWAYS.

TRAINS ON THE HARROGATE BRANCH OF THE YORK AND NORTH MIDLAND.

TO HARROGATE:

Miles.	STATIONS.	1 1, 2, and Gov.	2 1, 2, and 3 Class.	3 1, 2, and 3 Class.	4 1, 2, and 3 Class.	5 1, 2, and 3 Class.
	LEAVE	A. M.	A. M.	A. M.	P. M.	P. M.
	Manchester........	..	6 15	10 15	1 0	3 25
	London............	..	..	..	6 15	10 30
	Derby	..	6 0	9 20	12 30	4 0
	Normanton	7 20	10 0	12 30	3 20	6 25
	Newcastle..........	..	5 30	8 0	1 25	2 15
	Hull.......	6 20	8 35	10 20	1 35	5 0
	Leeds .:	7 20	9 50	12 30	2 55	6 0
	Scarborough.	..	7 0	9 0	12 30	4 20
	York	7 25	9 50	12 30	3 0	6 30
	Copmanthorpe......	7 33	..	12 38	3 8	6 38
	Bolton............	7 45	10 5	12 46	3 16	6 50
	Ulleskelf..........	7 50	..	12 49	3 20	6 55
	Church Fenton,....	8 30	11 0	1 30	4 10	7 13
	Stutton....Arrival at	8 36	11 6	1 36	4 16	7 19
	Tadcaster	8 40	11 10	1 40	4 20	7 20
	Newton...........	8 47	11 15	1 45	4 25	7 26
	Thorp Arch........	8 52	11 20	1 50	4 30	7 33
	Wetherby..........	8 58	11 25	1 55	4 35	7 38
	Spofforth..........	9 10	11 35	2 5	4 45	7 50
	Harrogate.:.......	9 25	11 50	2 20	5 0	8 5

FROM HARROGATE:

Miles.	STATIONS.	1 1, 2, and Gov.	2 1, 2, and 3 Class.	3 1, 2, and 3 Class.	4 1, 2, and 3 Class.	5 1, 2, and 3 Class.
	LEAVE	A. M.	A. M.	A. M.	P. M.	P. M.
	Harrogate..........	7 0	9 15	12 0	2 30	6 0
	Spofforth..........	7 15	9 30	12 15	2 45	6 15
	Wetherby...,.....	7 21	9 41	12 21	2 55	6 20
	Thorp Arch........	7 29	9 46	12 29	3 0	6 29
	Newton............	7 34	9 51	12 34	3 6	6 34
	Tadcaster .....,....	7 41	9 56	12 41	3 11	6 41
	Stutton	7 45	10 0	12 45	3 25	6 45
	Church Fenton.....	8 20	10 50	1 22	4 0	6 51
	Ulleskelf, Arrival at	8 26	10 56	1 28	4 6	7 10
	Bolton......	8 30	10 59	1 31	4 10	7 13
	Copmanthorpe......	8 40	11 3	1 40	4 18	7 22
	York.....'.Arrival at	8 50	11 20	1 50	4 25	7 30
	Scarborough........	11 15	2 0	5 30	5 30	..
	Leeds.............	8 55	11 20	1 50	4 30	8 0
	Hull.............	9 40	12 15	2 45	5 20	9 0
	Newcastle.........	12 45	3 20	6 0	8 5	11 0
	Normanton.........	8 40	11 0	..	4 25	8 20
	Derby	..	1 40	..	8 0	10 50
	London............	..	7 30	..	..	4 30
	Manchester.......	11 0	1 30	..	7 35	10 50

HARROGATE:—Printed and published by the Proprietor, PICKERSGILL PALLISER, at his General Printing Establishment, 31. Devonshire-Place.

Saturday, August 12, 1848.

From a lithograph by Gibson & Co., York. 1847.
THE CRIMPLE VIADUCT.

SEAL OF LEEDS NORTHERN RAILWAY COMPANY.

NORTH ENTRANCE OF BRAMHOPE TUNNEL.

The North Eastern Railway Company

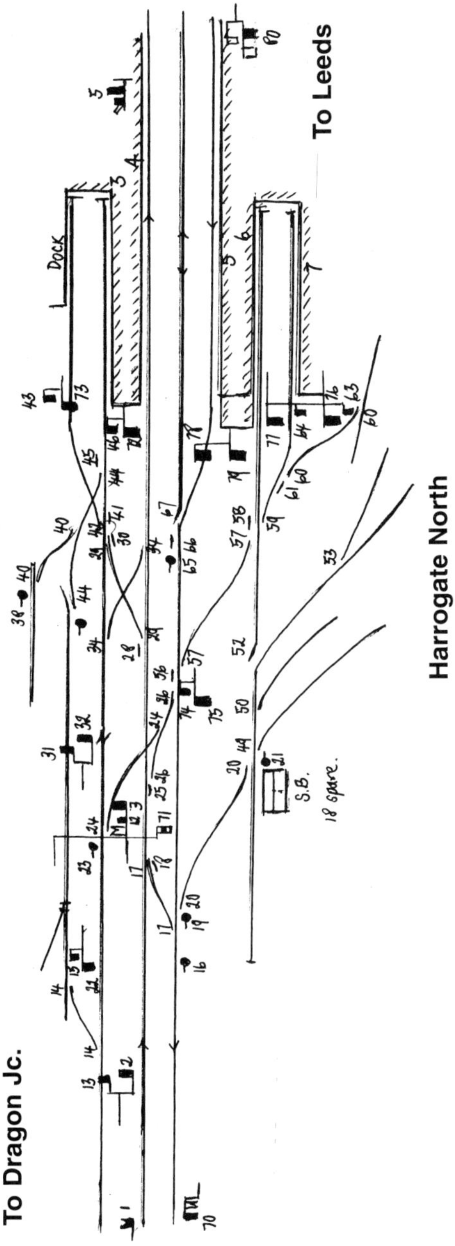
To Dragon Jc.
To Leeds
Harrogate North
Dock
S.B.
18 spare.

To Newcastle
Poppleton Jc.
To York

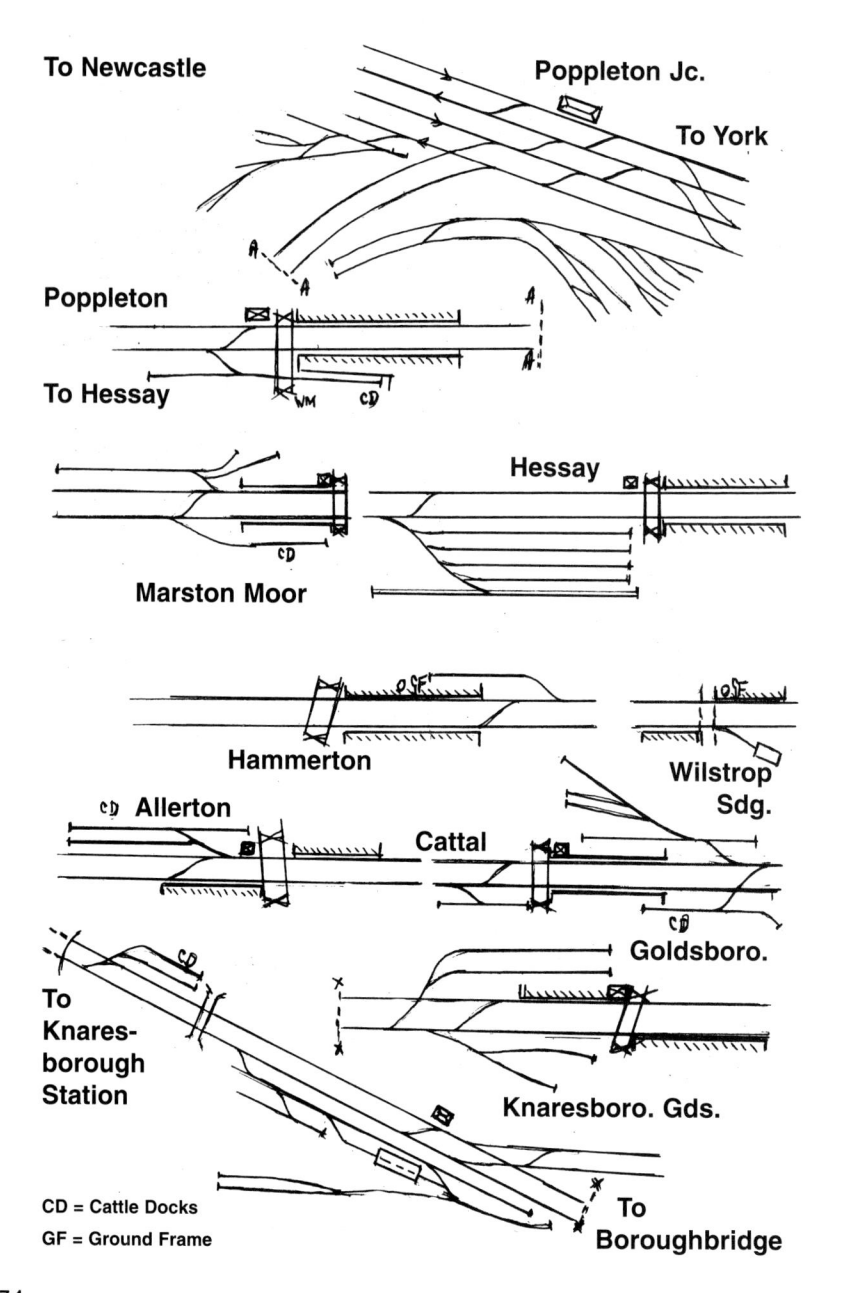

Poppleton
To Hessay

Hessay

Marston Moor

Hammerton
Wilstrop Sdg.

Allerton
Cattal

Goldsboro.

To Knaresborough Station

Knaresboro. Gds.

To Boroughbridge

CD = Cattle Docks
GF = Ground Frame

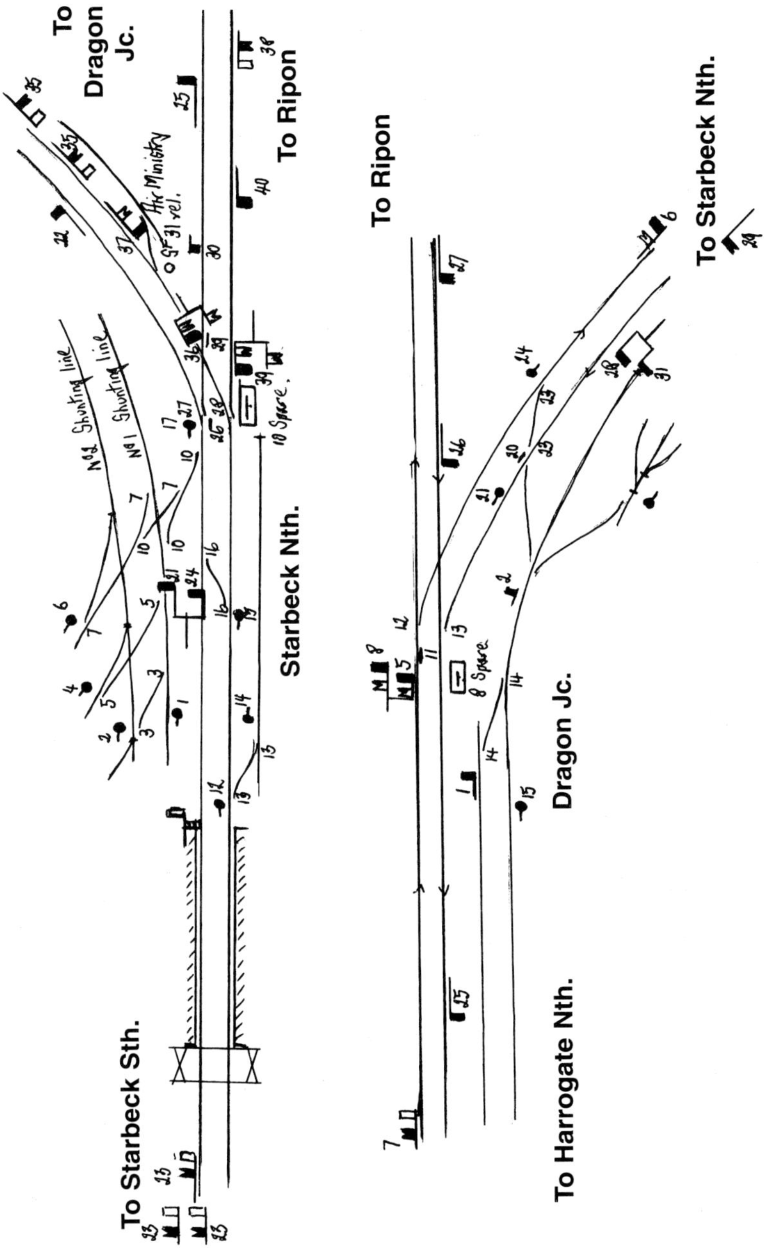
To Dragon Jc.
To Ripon
Starbeck Nth.
To Starbeck Sth.
No2 Shunting line
No1 Shunting line
Air Ministry
10 Spare
To Ripon
To Starbeck Nth.
Dragon Jc.
To Harrogate Nth.
8 Spare

Ref. 1002/AS 10,000—1-25

LONDON & NORTH EASTERN RAILWAY

P. 3183 (R)

.... Station. .... 19......

Form of Indemnity for Live Stock travelling loose in Horse Boxes

In consideration of your receiving and forwarding........................loose in Horse Box
(*No. and description of animals*)
not secured by the head in the ordinary manner, for conveyance by PASSENGER train from
........................Station to........................Station on the
........................, I agree to relieve the Company and all other Companies or persons
(*Date*)
over whose lines the animal/animals may pass or in whose possession same may be during any portion of the transit, from and against any loss arising from damage or injury caused by the said animal/animals during loading, transit, or unloading, except upon proof of wilful misconduct on the part of the Company or other Companies or their servants.

Signature of Sender or his Representative........................

Address ....

Witness to the above Signature this }
........................day of........................19........

LNER 668/1/45—50,000

P. 3632

London & North Eastern Railway

APPLICATION FOR SEASON TICKET

FOR OFFICE USE ONLY

Number of Ticket Issued } ....

PRICE

£   s.   d.

Season Tickets should be given up immediately they have expired. Persons using Season Tickets after date of expiry are liable to be prosecuted.

I, the undersigned, apply for a Season Ticket as follows:—

Name in full...
(Show Mr. Mrs. or Miss)

Address...

Class.................................

Period ....

Commencing Date ....

Expiry Date ....

Between...

and...

Ticket to be taken up at..Station.

If such Season Ticket is issued to me I hereby agree to accept the same or any renewal thereof upon the conditions printed on the other side.

Date.......................19........   Signature...

No. of Ticket now held.................. Date of issue.................. Expiry date..................

Please renew the Season Ticket each month or .... months until further notice.

Signed...

APPLICATIONS FOR SEASON TICKETS AT REDUCED RATES FOR PERSONS UNDER 18 YEARS OF AGE MUST BE MADE ON THE SPECIAL FORMS PROVIDED.

It is particularly requested that should any subsequent renewal of the Ticket not be required, notice thereof should be given to the Company at least 14 days before the expiry of the current Ticket.   [SEE BACK.

D 19—10,000—7-36. [W. & S. Ltd.]

London & North Eastern Railway.

Request for Passenger in Bath Chair to travel in Guard's Van.

P 3025

Form of Request to be signed by Passengers who require to travel in Bath Chairs, etc., in the Guard's Van.

To the London and North Eastern Railway Company and any other Railway Company concerned.

I request you to permit me* and *my attendant* to travel in the Guard's Van for a journey to be taken by me from_____Station to_____ Station on the_____day of_____19____, and in consideration of your so doing I undertake to release and indemnify you and each of you from all liability for loss of any kind or any injury occasioned to me* or *my attendant* or to my property* or *the property of my attendant*, during or consequent upon such journey.

Witness :   Dated this_____day of_____19

Name_____   Signature of Applicant_____

Address_____   Address_____

(*When the passenger is not accompanied by an attendant the words in italics must be erased.)

This form must be signed by the passenger, and must be retained at the Station at which the journey is commenced.

London & North Eastern Railway.

PERMIT TO TRAVEL IN GUARD'S VAN.

TO ALL CONCERNED.

The Bearer, M_____ having undertaken to release and indemnify the Company from all liability for loss of any kind or any injury occasioned to $\frac{him}{her}$* or to $\frac{his}{her}$ *attendant* during the journey has permission for $\frac{himself}{herself}$* and $\frac{his}{her}$ *attendant* to travel in the Guard's Van from_____Station to_____Station on the_____day of_____19____, upon and subject to the terms of the said undertaking.

Signature of Station Master_____

Office Stamp_____   Date_____19

(*When the passenger is not accompanied by an attendant the words in italics must be erased.)

This permit to be handed to the passenger who must produce it and give it up when required.

Est. 1005—A 2—25,000—3/25. P. 3121

LONDON & NORTH EASTERN RAILWAY.
APPLICATION FOR REDUCED FARE TICKETS.

TO THE
Booking Clerk,

_____ Station.

I request that tickets at reduced fares be supplied to the party of which particulars are given below, and the members of which are travelling together, outward and return.

Title of Party _____

	Adults.	Juveniles 16 to 18 years.	Juveniles 12 and under 16 years.	Children under 12 years.
Numbers of passengers for whom tickets required ...				

Travelling ... { From _____
{ To _____

Purpose of journey _____

Date of Outward Journey _____ Train Proposed _____

Date of Return Journey _____ do. _____

Signature of applicant _____

Address _____

Date of application _____

This form must be filled in and deposited with the Station Master or Agent at the Booking Station as early as possible before the date of travel when the arrangements will be confirmed, subject to the Train services and date proposed being suitable.

This space reserved for use of Booking Office.

Tickets issued :— Type _____ Nos. _____ Date _____

(*Signature of Station Master or Agent*).

Other publications by the same author:

'The Mexborough & Swinton Traction Company'.*
'The Burton & Ashby Light Railway'.
'Railways of South Yorkshire'.*
'The York & Scarborough Railway'.
'The Wakefield, Pontefract & Goole Railway'.
'The Railways of Castleford'.
'Huddersfield Branch Lines'.
'The Railways of Hull'.*
'The Selby & Driffield Railway'.
'To the Crystal Palace'. (Forge Books)
'To the Alexandra Palace'. (Forge Books)
'Trentham, the Gardens and Branch Railway'.*
'Doncaster's Trams & Trolleybuses'.
'The Dearn District Light Railway'.
'The Selby & Goole Railway'. (Oakwood)*
'The Wensleydale Branch'. (Oakwood)*
'The Hertford Loop'. (Oakwood)
'Railways of East Yorkshire'. (Oakwood)*
'Railways of North Lincs.'
'The Hull & Scarborough Railway'.

(* denotes those that are out of print but which may be in stock or available in libraries).